"To read *Living Big* is a delight, and to put its principles into practice is downright thrilling."

—VICTORIA MORAN, author of *Lit from Within* and *Creating a Charmed Life*

"With this inspiring book, Pam Grout blows the lid off your limited thinking and invites you to become extraordinary. Turn off the TV, she advises, reclaim your personal power, and start spinning miracles."

—GAIL MCMEEKIN, M.S.W., author of *The Power of Positive Choices* and *The 12 Secrets of Highly Creative Women*

"A brilliant, enticing guide to a life of adventure and purpose. Let Pam Grout escort, enthrall and, yes, nudge you, into creating a life you thought you could only dream of."

—FATHER PAUL KEENAN, author of *Stages of the Soul* and *Heartstorming*

"If you long to live a life of passion and purpose but wonder where to begin, stop right now and read Pam Grout's wonderful and dynamic book *Living Big*. Pam writes from the bone and speaks from her heart. She knows what it means to find and then follow your joy. Take Pam on your journey and embrace what really matters."

—LESLIE LEVINE, author of *Ice Cream for Breakfast: If You Follow All the Rules, You Miss Half the Fun*

Living Big

Embrace Your Passion and
LEAP into an Extraordinary Life

PAM GROUT

CONARI PRESS
Berkeley, California

Conari Press books are distributed by Publishers Group West.

ISBN: 1-57324-703-0

Cover Illustration/Photography: © Image Bank, Packert White
Cover Design: Suzanne Albertson
Author Photo: Ron Dewitt
Interior Design and Composition: Nancy Campana, Campana Design

Library of Congress Cataloging-in-Publication Data

Grout, Pam.
Living big : embrace your passion and leap into an
extraordinary life / Pam Grout.
p.   cm.
ISBN 1-57324-703-0
1. Quality of life. 2. Conduct of life. 3. Quality of life—Case
studies. 4. Conduct of life—Case studies. I. Title.
BF637.C5 G77 2001
158—dc21
                                        2001003066

Printed in Canada on recycled paper.
01 02 03 04   TR   10 9 8 7 6 5 4 3 2 1

This one's for Ronnie.

LIFE IS TOO SHORT TO BE LITTLE.

—*Disraeli*

This is a book of magic.

Sign your name here if you're ready for a life of enchantment, mystery, wonder, and passion:

_____

You *(yoo)* 1: The person whose name is signed on this line 2: Immense 3: Vast 4: Endless 5: Colossal 6: Enormous 7: Boundless 8: Astronomical 9: Tremendous 10: Infinite 11: Mammoth 12: Mastodonic 13: Gigantic 14: Gargantuan 15: Herculean 16: Humongous 17: Prodigious 18: Stupendous 19: Cosmic 20: Whopping 21: Thunderous 22: Larger than life

LIVING BIG

What's the Big Idea? 1

You Were Created to Do Big Things 21

1 / Thinking Big: The Attitude of Boldness 25

2 / Giving Big: The Attitude of Service 45

3 / Blessing Big: The Attitude of Kindness 69

4 / Making a Big Difference: The Attitude of Commitment 91

5 / Imagining Big: The Attitude of Creativity 111

6 / Playing Big: The Attitude of Happiness 135

7 / Loving Big: The Attitude of Spirituality 159

Wrapping Up with a Big Bang 177

Acknowledgments 179

About the Author 181

WHAT'S THE BIG IDEA?

EVERY DAY, YOU ARE SIGNALED AND SUMMONED TO
EMBARK ON A JOURNEY BEYOND THE BOUNDARIES OF ALL
YOU HAVE EVER KNOWN. YOU NEED ONLY RELINQUISH
YOUR FEARS, OPEN YOUR HEART AND BEGIN.

—*Bob Savino,* As the Spirit Moves

The average human being squanders his imagination, hoards her love, and has no clue about the depths that exist within his own soul.

Or, as the great poet Ranier Maria Rilke put it, "Most people come to know only one corner of their room, one narrow strip on which they keep walking back and forth."

Living Big is about discovering the rest of your room.

We all know the pitiful statistic about our brainpower: that we use a scant 10 percent of what's available. What's worse is we use even less of our love, acknowledge only a fraction of our feelings, and cower in the face of our highest dreams.

If you ask me, the reason five out of ten people in this country hate their jobs and 17 million are clinically depressed is that they're leading lives that are "way beneath them." They're exhausting themselves on meaningless things.

Scientists estimate the average human being has 60,000 thoughts a day. A pretty impressive statistic until you hear this one: All but 2 percent of those 60,000 thoughts are the same ones you had yesterday.

Just think what we could do if we used that other 98 percent to think up new ideas, to dive into life's mysteries, to solve the problems that face our world? Most of us waste our 60,000 thoughts on trivial, insignificant, thoroughly meaningless things. Look at the cover of a typical woman's magazine:

"Lose 5 Pounds by Christmas"

"101 Ways to Regain Your Energy"

"Drive Your Lover Wild in Bed"

Don't we have anything better to read about? If the 7 million readers of *Ladies' Home Journal* would all wonder instead, "What can I do to improve my own soul?" or, "How could I make our schools more loving?" the big problems we're so afraid of would be solved in a year. Seven million people focusing on issues like that would be an unstoppable force.

But instead we focus on absurd trivialities. We live at half-throttle. We suit up for hopscotch when we could be performing miracles. We're completely oblivious to our own majesty, to the fact that the very heartbeat of the Divine thrums through our veins. Instead of greeting each day with our holy gifts, we pound on the snooze button, desperate for fifteen more minutes. Therein lies the source of all our problems.

Living Big is a book about hooking into the other 90 percent of our brains, loving with every ounce of our souls, stepping up to claim our wildest dreams.

I used to think a big life meant getting on *The Late Show with David Letterman.* I used to worry I'd never find anything to inspire producers to call directory assistance for my number. I knew good and well I'd never be an actor, the odds of me making the Olympics were about 285 million to 1, and my pets, despite my insistent coaching, could never seem to master any stupid pet tricks.

And then I realized that many of the people on the talk show circuit, while certainly glamorous, are probably not any bigger than the Great and Terrible Oz once you actually peek behind the curtain. Yes, some of the TV actors we idolize are living big lives, but many of them are just as small and scared as the rest of us. And on the same token, there are hundreds of people whose names you've never heard of who are living giant, Titanic-sized lives.

So among other things, *Living Big* is a book of stories. It's about ordinary people who are doing extraordinary things. It's about visionaries, dreamers, people who discarded the cushy and glamorous for a more meaningful vision. People who are on a crusade.

Some of the people in this book are out to save the world—to clean up polluted oceans, to preserve ancient cultures, to administer CPR to antiquated political systems. Others long to introduce adventure and spirit to a society that has practically forgotten how to smile. Still others just want to have peace. But no matter what the mission, no matter what the vision, the people in this book all know that life is to be cherished, that "No" is never the right answer, and that one person can make a difference. Or at least an awfully big dent.

And while *Living Big* may appear to be a book about heroes, about *other* people, it's also a book about you. About what's possible within you.

The people in this book haven't done anything you can't do. It's important to remember that. These people who live big simply took their gifts and put them to use. It is my hope that their inspiration will be the foundation for your own Big Life. That their passion will inspire you to find your own purpose, your own mission in life.

All of us have one.

The first step to Living Big is simple awareness, realizing it *is* possible, acknowledging that time and time again, human beings have risen above their limitations to achieve extraordinary things.

SO WHAT DOES
LIVING BIG MEAN ANYWAY?

Living Big isn't about making lots of money or having a Texas-sized house. It's about having an intoxicating vision, about daring to look at the miracle of life without shrinking back. Living Big means having the nerve to find your own drum beat, sing your own song.

Unfortunately, many of us still march to the same high school fight song we learned decades ago. Or we sing the same old jingle that Madison Avenue invented to keep us buying their products. In case you hadn't noticed, there are an awful lot of forces out there striving to keep us in line.

Living Big means getting out of line. It means dancing the jig while others are waltzing. It means saying you care when you're not sure how the other person feels. It means leaping out of the limited, soul-numbing boxes we've all been squeezed into.

Living Big is being brave enough to claim your own truth, being bold enough to read the poem that's stamped across your heart. Out loud so everybody can hear.

All of us have the responsibility to find that passion that makes us want to get up on the table and dance. Walt Whitman once said that every man's job was to write his own bible. My dream for *Living Big* is that each and every one of you will not only write your own bible, but your own autobiography and your own wish list of dreams.

Because, quite frankly, I want to know who you are.

Yes, you're wearing the same black leather jacket that everyone else is wearing this season, and you're riding the same scooter that everyone else is riding, but who are you underneath all that? What is the thing that makes you want to jump off the chair and scream with unmitigated joy?

I need to know. But more important, you need to tell. We all do. So the steps to Living Big are pretty simple:

1. Find your passion.
2. Follow it.

Instead of saying *find* your passion, I should probably say *own* your passion, embrace it, kiss it like a long-lost relative. So many of us think we have to find it, that it's *out there* somewhere, this thing that would make us happy. But engraved on your very soul is the already written script for your passion. It's not a matter of going anywhere to find it. Or reading some book that will tell you how to claim it. It's about taking off the layers and observing what has always been there.

You know you're getting close when you feel a little buzz, when the thought of it makes you really, really excited.

That's not to say you won't get scared. Or you won't feel like hiding under the bed when the time comes to act on your idea. Fear is practically a spiritual prerequisite. I remember telling a friend that for me to write a book about Living Big was akin to me writing a book about Newtonian physics. But then I thought to myself, "What do I want more than anything else in the world?"

To live big. To claim my destiny.

Yes, there's this insistent impostor who's always trying to convince me I'm insignificant, that my ideas will never matter. But there's also this other voice. And it knows better.

That's the other part of Living Big—making a difference. All my life I've made noises about wanting my life to serve a bigger purpose.

It is my highest hope that this book will make some kind of impact on the world's consciousness. If we stay in the restrictive ruts we're in now, we will never solve the world's problems. And there are a lot of problems that need solving, a lot of big things that need doing.

We have kids taking guns to school. We have mass destruction of our rain forests. We have neighbors so lonely that Jay Leno is their only friend.

So I have to ask, What are we going to do about it? No longer can we sit back, finger our remotes, and say, "Tut, tut, what a shame." We must act. We must grow out of our wimpy, apathetic, small lives and take action. Any kind of action.

As long as there is prejudice, environmental destruction, people calling each other names, there is something big to do. We don't have the right or the luxury to be small.

The answer to your problems and the world's problems are one and the same.

And that answer is you. Us. Now.

CHANGE YOUR ATTITUDE.
CHANGE YOUR LIFE.

THE GREATEST DISCOVERY OF MY GENERATION IS
THAT HUMAN BEINGS CAN ALTER THEIR LIVES BY
ALTERING THEIR ATTITUDES OF MIND.

—*William James*

The size of our life, essentially, is the result of our attitudes. Our attitudes affect everything from our relationships to our health to our mindset while doing a crossword puzzle. If we're going to embrace our passion and live big, we must grow our attitudes.

Unfortunately, most of us live with attitudes that confine us. Attitudes that keep us small. As the great humanist Buckminster Fuller said, "We are powerfully imprisoned by the terms in which we have been conducted to think."

We adopted most of our attitudes without consent. We picked them up from our families or our culture or that ubiquitous, "They say." It never even occurred to us that we could choose a different set of attitudes.

We can.

The first attitude we must adopt is that our life is up to us. We must take responsibility for designing our own lives.

Most of us believe our main job in life is to set boundaries, to figure out what isn't working and then to get rid of it.

People who do us wrong?

Gone.

Parents who didn't act like Ward and June Cleaver?

Out the window.

This attitude totally negates who we are. It's like signing the papers to a new house, walking in the front door, and then storming out because there isn't any furniture. There's only one person who can furnish the house. It's up to you to create the kind of life you want.

So often we get indignant while we're looking at our lives and say, "I deserve much better than this." And you're right. You do. But it is *your responsibility* and only your responsibility to create "much better than this."

Yes, you may be in a relationship that isn't loving. You may have a job that doesn't trip your trigger. But who is the one and only person with the power to change those things?

Calling out a search party for the next guy, the next job, the next self-help book is like calling in the fire department to blow out the candles on your birthday cake. You don't need the fire department. You don't even need a candle extinguisher. You have the power to blow out your own candles. You have the power to fix every single thing that's not working in your life. First you have to grow your attitude.

John F. Kennedy posed an oft-quoted challenge to the citizens of America: "Ask not what your country can do for you, but what you can do for your country." This is the essence of Living Big. Ask not what your life can do for you, but what you can do for your life. Living Big means looking for the potential in what's already there. It means saying to yourself, "I accept what I have. And here's what I can do with it."

Quit looking. Take what you have now. Take the relationships you have now. Take the job you have now. Take the home you have now. And turn them into something beautiful.

We must take back our power. We must say, "I am a loving person, a strong, mighty person, and there is nothing in my life that cannot be restored to wholeness. And it's up to me—and only me—to see that this happens."

HOW IT WORKS

ILLUSIONS MISTAKEN FOR
TRUTH ARE THE PAVEMENT UNDER OUR FEET.

—*Barbara Kingsolver,* Poisonwood Bible

In the chapters that follow, I'm going to present seven BIG attitudes that are second nature to People Who Live Big. The good news is, these are all attitudes you *used* to have. They're attitudes from your childhood, attitudes that are hard-wired into your very being.

Living Big makes the argument that these childhood attitudes are the big, important things in life—the attitudes we had before we learned it was wrong to jump on the bed.

Let's go back to our childhoods, when anything was possible. Back before we learned to "wipe that silly grin off" our face, before we were told to "watch out," "be careful," "avoid strangers." Other than the bit about drinking eight glasses of water a day, most of what "they say" is wrong. Or at least irrelevant, unnecessary, and unproductive for growing a big life.

Marianne Williamson tells the story of a little girl who showed her teacher a picture she had painted of a purple tree. The teacher, said, "Sweetheart, I've never seen a purple tree, now have I?"

"That's too bad," said the little girl. "That's really too bad."

And while it's "too bad" that you, too, might have forgotten about purple trees and the unfathomable depths within you, it's "really good" that you're here now, ready to remember.

1. Thinking Big: The Attitude of Boldness, or why it's not necessary to "be careful." By the time we start grade school, most of us have heard the phrase "Be careful" at least 10,000 times. It's practically a mother's moral imperative to utter that warning every time her kid jumps on a jungle gym, joins a soccer team, or pursues the boy she has a big crush on.

Instead, we should urge our kids to throw caution to the wind.

"Get out there."

"Take risks."

"Fall flat on your face."

Being careful gets us nowhere. If Martin Luther King, Jr., had been careful, he'd have never had a dream that someday people would not be judged by the color of their skin. If Christopher Columbus had been careful, he'd have never made it to the New World. Hey, as far as his parents knew, the world was flat and he was at great risk for falling off the edge.

The first attitude of Living Big is Thinking Big, or the Attitude of Boldness. People Who Live Big are not careful. They don't settle. They do not feel obligated to do things just because their parents did. Or because the Joneses did. People Who Live Big don't care what anybody else thinks. They, as Nike likes to say, "just do it!"

2. Giving Big: The Attitude of Service, or why it's unnecessary to "always look out for number one." "They say" it's important to watch our backs, to protect our own space. But ironically enough, the defining moment, the turning point for each of the Big People profiled in this book was the moment they finally decided to "get over themselves." Andrea Campbell met twenty deformed kids from Russia while sitting in a doctor's office and realized, "Whoa, what do I have to worry about?" For Patch Adams, it was having empathy for a lonely guy who had no friends. James Twyman got over himself by working with homeless AIDS victims.

The second attitude of Living Big is Giving Big, or the Attitude of Service. It's being able to give everything you've got without the slightest thought of recompense. You don't have to have a big intellect or a great talent to be a giant. But you must rise above the mediocre thinking that insists it's only prudent to "look out for number one."

3. Blessing Big: The Attitude of Kindness, or why you should "always speak to strangers." From the time we're old enough to toddle away, we've been told we should avoid people we don't know. "They say" it's prudent to be cautious until we get a letter of recommendation.

After all, they say, "There are lots of crazies out there."

But you know what? 99.9 percent of all the people in this world are really nice. For every loony bin that makes the news, there are 5,000 people who would gladly give you the coat off their back. By being suspicious, distrustful, unwilling to talk to strangers, we promote suspiciousness and distrust, plus we miss out on a huge group of wonderful friends.

So I say, "Speak to strangers."

In fact, speak until there *are* no strangers.

If you need a letter of recommendation,
feel free to use this one from me.

Letter of
Recommendation for

_____

(You can fill in the blank for every Tom, Dick and Harry on this planet. I don't care if the person is homeless, crippled, or wearing a black and white prison uniform.)

_____ is a good person. Given a little love, a little understanding, he/she will do remarkable things.

Sure, he/she has probably made a few mistakes, probably done a few stupid things. But, boy, does he/she have a lot of love to give, a lot of ideas that can change the world.

By all means, take this person into your heart.

"Hire him/her" as your friend and confidante at your earliest possible convenience. Do not wait. Do not hesitate. There is nothing to be afraid of. This person is a treasure.

Sincerely yours,

Pam Grout

The third attitude of Living Big is Blessing Big, or the Attitude of Kindness. It means connecting with other people. Spreading love and goodness. Each of us is assigned a plot in the big cosmic garden. We can either tend it kindly and joyously, or we can watch mindlessly while it grows weeds.

4. Making a Big Difference: The Attitude of Commitment, or why you should never "just sit there and watch TV." This is probably the biggest deterrent to living a full, joyful life. Passivity.

We have become viewers instead of doers. Recent studies show that the average American is three to four times more likely to watch TV on any given evening than to talk with family and friends. The typical American father spends ten minutes a day talking to his children. Time in front of the TV? Four to six hours. That's more than a third of our waking lives. No offense, but it takes more skill to brush your teeth than it does to watch TV.

Slowly, over time, we have given up our inheritance. We have turned over our power to think for ourselves, to make things up, to imagine, to plan, and to dream. Inside each and every one of us is a master chef, an inventor, a writer, a leader. All these heroes, these immense giants that exist within our souls, are sick to death of watching "Days of Our Lives."

Sure, we may know about every famine that hits Africa, the scores of every sporting event, and every nuance of the latest crime. But what do we do about it?

"Just sit there and watch TV."

An Amish woman in southern Pennsylvania once told a pollster who asked about modern conveniences, "We don't want TV because it would keep us from visiting our neighbors. How can we care for each other if we do not know our neighbors?"

The fourth component of Living Big is Making a Big Difference, or the Attitude of Commitment. It means taking up a cause, leaving a legacy. It means standing up and taking action, believing in the power of one person to make a difference.

5. Imagining Big: The Attitude of Creativity, or why you should never "stay in line." The only problem with this often-heard piece of advice is that nobody knows where the line is. And anybody who pretends to is, at best, showing you his or her own line. Which is fine for them. But it's not your line. Pretty much anything is possible, and you are free to adapt any guidelines you choose. But *there is no line.*

French naturalist John Henry Fabre did an interesting experiment with processionary caterpillars. Their name should pretty much give them away: They get in a line and blindly follow the procession. It doesn't matter if the leader is heading over a cliff or under a car tire. The good little caterpillars stay in line. Fabre filled a large flower pot with dirt. Around the rim, he placed fifteen processionary caterpillars. Sure enough, they followed each other, around and around the circle, until it was impossible to tell which was the leader and which were the followers.

In the center of the flower pot, he put a plentiful supply of pine needles, the caterpillar's main food source. Unfortunately, the caterpillars marched around and around for seven days and seven nights until they finally keeled over from starvation and exhaustion.

I think that's what we've done. We've lost track of who is the leader and who is the follower. I don't mean to point fingers, but maybe staying in line is leading us to a bland, exhausting, and spiritually starved march toward nothingness. We need to get out of our line and express who we really are.

The fifth attitude of Living Big is Imagining Big, or the Attitude of Creativity. On the day you were born, God presented you with a creative gift. It is a gift the world needs. Imagining

Big means being open to the magic, the deep vistas that fill up your soul.

6. Playing Big: The Attitude of Happiness, or why you should never "wipe that silly grin off your face." "They say" we should not allow ourselves to be sidetracked with goofiness. Our job is to "do our job" and to "contribute to the growth of our nation."

Silliness, they say, is a waste of valuable time.

To that, I say, "Lo-to-to." In fact, we need *more* silliness, more willingness to look like a crackpot.

The word *silly* was originally a Middle English word, *sillig,* that meant "blessing." If all of us were willing to do three silly things a day, things like wear our coats backward or yodel on traffic-jammed freeways, we would unquestionably receive more blessings. We would be freer to break new paths, find new adventures. As People Who Live Big, we are not here to do what has already been done.

Maybe all of us should loosen up a bit and hitch our dreams to a sillier star.

The sixth attitude of Living Big is Playing Big, or what I call the Attitude of Happiness. It means seeing life as a grand adventure, viewing each day as an unusual and exciting experience.

7. Loving Big: The Attitude of Spirituality, or why it really doesn't matter if you "always wear clean underwear." There's just one problem with this bit of well-meaning advice. Clean underwear focuses on material things. It insinuates that if you have the right underwear or the right furniture or the right car that somehow life will be smoother. Material things, in case you haven't figured out by now, do not make us happy.

In fact, I would hazard to say that our blind chase for the

material is what makes us so unhappy and so stressed. It doesn't make a bit of difference what kind of underwear you're wearing. The only things that matters are what dreams are written on your heart and how much compassion and love can you spread to your fellow man.

The last attitude of Living Big is Loving Big, or the Attitude of Spirituality. You're not doing anyone any favors when you play small. Loving Big means recognizing who you are and why you're here.

THERE'S MORE....

For each attitude, I've included three sections: profiles of People Who Live Big (heretofore known as PLBs), 3 Big Questions, and Boot Camp for the Soul.

People Who Live Big

NEVER DOUBT THAT A SMALL GROUP OF COMMITTED CITIZENS CAN CHANGE THE WORLD. INDEED, IT'S THE ONLY THING THAT EVER HAS.

—*Margaret Mead*

People who want to paint study Picasso. People who want to play piano study Mozart. Those of us who want to live big, well, we're going to study PLBs (People Who Live Big).

Throughout history, there have been thousands of people who have summoned the courage to follow a personal vision.

People like Mary Colter, a revolutionary architect who began her career in 1902, eighteen years before women had even received the right to vote. People like Osseola McCarty, a Mississippi washerwoman, who raised hundreds of thousands of dollars for scholarships for African American kids who might otherwise not have gone to college. People like Jimmie Davis, who in his short 101 years, was governor of Louisiana and a successful country and western songwriter. People like C. J. Walker, who became the country's first female millionaire by making and selling hair products.

To live big is to join a powerful brotherhood. It's to come face to face with Joan of Arc, Michael Jordan, Eric Clapton. It's to take on the cloak of Shakespeare, Rumi, and Oprah Winfrey, who said, "I always knew I was a hit record just waiting to happen." It's to join a proud circle with many members from all places and times.

The PLBs you'll find in this book are all living today. They're people I've run across in my work as a journalist. Some of them I know personally. Some of them I've profiled for magazines. Some of them I've just followed because they inspire me to "make my life extraordinary."

All of them are excellent models of what is possible. Scientists know the importance of role models in learning and behavior. A semanticist named Alfred Korzybski called this unique ability to learn from others "time-binding." The knowledge gained by others binds us all together; if one person can do it, the rest of us can, too.

You've probably heard of the Hundredth Monkey Theory. It seems that monkeys on a remote island mastered a new method of getting bananas down from trees. Before long, monkeys on other islands began retrieving bananas the same way, even though they'd had no physical contact with the monkeys who'd first mastered the technique. The theory is that if enough members of a group (in this instance, a hundred monkeys) acquire a new piece of knowledge or a new skill, it will pass into the collective unconscious and all members will acquire it.

When one of us turns up the voltage, all of us see more clearly.

Those who can tap quickly into the knowledge of others and who can acquire new skills, attitudes, and behaviors have a critical advantage in life. Martin Luther King, Jr., studied the life of Gandhi. Gandhi took many of his great ideas from Tolstoy. Robert E. Lee patterned himself after George Washington. The Wright Brothers received their inspiration while reading about a French inventor. John Wooden, former basketball coach for UCLA, says Ward "Piggy" Lambert of Purdue University taught him everything he knew. Einstein learned from Newton, and Newton learned from Galileo. It goes on and on.

We are all connected. Maybe your decision to live big will be the one decision that tips the scales. Maybe you're the hundredth monkey.

3 Big Questions

SEEK THE HIGHEST THAT IS IN YOU.

—*Lundbergh*

Sam Keen once said that the quality of our lives is in direct proportion to the questions we ask. If we ask important questions, we'll get important answers. The universe will match us question for question, will answer whatever it is we ask.

So why not ask big questions, think big thoughts? We must ask, "What if?" on a daily basis.

Instead of, "How can I stretch this paycheck to the end of the month?" we should ask, "What can I give that would make me sing with joy?"

Instead of, "What's the closing price on Janus Worldwide?" or, "How much is the shank loin at Safeway?" we can ask, "How can I grow into the loving, wise, inspiring person I am meant to be?"

With each Big Attitude, I'm going to ask three Big Questions, questions I call miracle questions. I urge you to spend time pondering these Big Questions.

Anything is possible, but we have to imagine it first. The more big questions we ask, the more we dare to say, "What would it look like if?" the bigger we will become. Putting your attention on something calls it into existence. We can literally reshape and redesign our lives by asking bigger questions.

Boot Camp for the Soul

TO CHANGE YOUR LIFE: START IMMEDIATELY;
DO IT FLAMBOYANTLY; NO EXCEPTIONS.

—*William James*

I know what you're thinking. You wanted to *read* a book, have something to stick on your *bookshelf.* But if you really want to live big, you have to take action. You have to *do* something.

In fact, the main problem with inspirational books (and, yes, that includes this one) is they're undertaken while sitting down. The only thing they require is *mental* activity.

Now, don't get me wrong. A rich, deep mental life is key number one to a big life. But once you start asking and answering the big questions, you can't help but stand up and actually be a bigger person. Living Big by definition means taking action.

But here's the good news. Boot Camp for the Soul, if practiced with discipline, is guaranteed to peel the calluses off your heart. It's guaranteed to modify any and all small-minded behavior. Follow the simple actions suggested at the end of each chapter for the number of days suggested and you'll be lifted once and for all out of worn-down old ruts.

As your drill sergeant, I must warn you: Boot Camp for the Soul has some pretty "in-your-face" requirements. At first, they might look, well, a bit outrageous. Yet, they're not. All of these Boot Camp exercises are things we should be doing anyway, things we shouldn't need a book to remind us of. Some of them will be sheer terror at first. I mean, who wants to break out of old patterns, especially if it means talking to strangers and embarrassing yourself in public? But I guarantee that if you follow through, dullness and boredom will melt away. Your life will become joyous and fun. You will become a PLB.

There's nothing the average person can't do. In fact, the big surprise is that the average person isn't doing these things already.

Nothing in Boot Camp costs a penny. None of it takes much time. You don't even have to get up at 0500 hours. All it takes is a slight bit of willingness to do some things that might be termed "out of the ordinary."

But, hey, that's what we're sick of. Being ordinary.

Yes, I know you'd probably rather write some more affirmations, visualize some more goals, and speak some more positive thoughts.

But Living Big is a whole different brand of cereal. It's definitely not, as the commercials say, your mother's Oldsmobile.

But take heart. Once you break out, once you complete basic training, you will be so incredibly amazed at the "you" that you are that you'll wonder why you didn't do this ten years ago.

Trust me on this one. You will never be happier, more energized, or more sure about who you are. Great freedom comes in taking risks, stepping outside that tiny little line that society prescribes as "normal."

So that's Living Big in a nutshell.

Might as well buckle your seatbelts. Or better yet. Unbuckle them. Unroll the windows. Scream out at the top of your lungs, "Hey world! Here I am! And I am ready to live B-I-G exclamation point!"

It's about time for the ride of your life.

YOU WERE CREATED
TO DO BIG THINGS

LIVE YOUR BELIEFS AND YOU
CAN TURN THE WORLD AROUND.

—Henry David Thoreau

When you were born, you were powerfully connected to a rich, deep world, a world of magic and enchantment. You could do anything.

But then your parents got ahold of you.

"It's wrong to speak your mind," crazy to talk to the angels, ridiculous to think you could be a painter.

Why did you believe them?

Pablo Casals, the famous cellist, once said,

> Each second we live in a new and unique moment of the universe, a moment that never was before and will never be again. And what do we teach our children in school? We teach them that two and two makes four, and that Paris is the capital of France. When will we also teach them what they are?
>
> We should say to each of them: You are a marvel. You are unique. In all the world there is no other child exactly like you. In the millions of years that have passed there has never been a child like you. You may become a Shakespeare, a Michelangelo, a Beethoven. You have the capacity for anything.

In other words, you are not here to "get by."

You are here to create the good, the beautiful, and the holy.

You're here to dance, to spread love, to write symphonies, to give birth to the very best that is inside of you. You are here on this planet to love big. To think big thoughts, to dream big dreams.

Those dysfunctional families that you love to go on and on about? You can heal them.

The crime? The overcrowding? The greed that so pervades our culture? You can change it.

You have that kind of power. But you have forgotten. You've squandered your power on meaningless things. You've bartered it away for security. You've wasted your talent by not trusting it. You've hidden your individuality for a paycheck.

There's a very wise tribe in South America. When someone in their village does something wrong—like steal a neighbor's papaya—the village gathers in a very important tribal meeting. They take the offender, place him in the middle of a circle, and begin to tell wonderful stories about him, stories from his childhood, stories that honor who he is. Remember that time that Kunta climbed the coconut tree faster than anyone else? Remember the time he made that seashell necklace for his grandmother? To them, it's obvious that if he is stealing papayas he has forgotten who he is.

That's what most of us have done. We have forgotten who we are. So now, we're going to put you in a tribal circle and remind you.

1. You are a precious child, loved beyond your wildest imagination by the Creator of all things.

2. You are a one-of-a-kind miracle, a priceless treasure. You have qualities in mind, speech, movement, and appearance like no one who has ever lived. In all the 78 billion humans who have walked this planet, not one has even had the same fingerprint. Nor will there ever be another like you.

3. You have the power and the ability to make a huge difference in this world. In fact, your contribution is one that no one else will be able to make.

4. Your mind is capable of coming up with incredible, Earth-shattering ideas. They are ideas the world needs.

5. You have at least one idea that can save the world.

6. You have two jobs. The first is to discover and sing your own song. The second is to spread love. Both will entail dancing.

7. Every cell in your body radiates love. Your smile can brighten a room. Your words can inspire someone to forgive instead of kill. You have the ability to turn fear into hope, horror into peace. You can uplift the despondent, cheer the unhappy, warm the lonely, and encourage the defeated. This is your responsibility as a human being on this planet.

8. You are a miracle worker. If miracles are not a part of your day-to-day experience, something has gone wrong.

9. You are a champion in a championship game.

10. The world is watching and waiting to applaud.

CHAPTER 1

Thinking Big:
The Attitude
of Boldness

NOT TO DREAM MORE BOLDLY MAY
TURN OUT TO BE, IN VIEW OF PRESENT
REALITIES, SIMPLY IRRESPONSIBLE.

—George Leonard

hen you were five, you *knew* you were the Queen of Sheba. There was no doubt in your mind that you were going to do big things, that your life was important. You paraded around like the gallant human being that you are, driving your parents crazy with your "Mommy, mommy, look at me's."

Unfortunately, at some point between the ages of seven and thirteen, most of us shut down and decide to go shopping.

Living Big means regaining that five-year-old audacity. It means finding the gall to stand up and say, "Hey, over here." You've got to be bold in your actions. Outrageous in your dreams. And to remember that you are capable of anything. Believing anything else is denying who you are.

Some might protest that boldness is impudent, that being modest is the attribute to strive for. But modesty is nothing but a learned affectation.

Robert Fulghum's now-famous essay, *All I Really Need to Know I Learned in Kindergarten,* was recently made into a stage play. In one of the first scenes, the kindergarten teacher asks her fresh young students how many of them are dancers:

"I am. I am," they all shout exuberantly.

"And how many of you are singers?" she continues.

Again, all of them wave their hands wildly.

"Painters?"

Unanimous hand-waving.

"Writers?

More unanimous hand-waving.

In fourth grade, another teacher asks the same questions of the same students. Now, only a third of the students are dancers, singers, painters, writers. By high school, the number who are willing to claim artistic talent is down to a paltry handful. Where did the confidence and enthusiasm go?

Some well-meaning parent or teacher probably told them they were not painters. Some aptitude test with a fancy title gave an official score that said they had better give up that misguided ambition of being a writer. Try accounting. Some guidance counselor broke the news that only a chosen few have artistic talent.

Very early on, we turn over the reins to something outside ourselves. The coach tells us if we're good enough to be on the basketball team. The music teacher tells us if we have the talent to sing in the choir. Our teachers give us arbitrary grades that tell us if we're smart enough to make the honor role, bright enough to get into college.

Our art teachers give us the rules: Grass is green, skies are blue.

Why did we listen? How can anybody else know what color your grass is? How can anybody else know what notes you're supposed to sing? They know what's right for them. But they haven't a clue what is right for you.

Only you know that. And you do know. You don't need another workshop, another book, another psychic reading.

By stepping forward—even when you're not sure you're ready—you'll find genius, power, and magic. Your way will become clear. Oftentimes, we're foggy about our purpose, not quite sure what we want, and it's only because we've been too timid to stick our necks out.

When we're bold, when we challenge the status quo—both in ourselves and in others—the answers to all our questions will gallop in on charging stallions.

Being bold is a simple matter of claiming your inheritance. Saying, "Hey look what I can do!" is simple acknowledgment of who you are.

I am not great because I am Pam Grout, an author, a tennis player, a 5 foot 10 inch mother from Kansas. I am great because I am a human being, part of a proud and noble tribe that includes Gandhi, Shakespeare, and Martin Luther King, Jr. The same heartbeat that pulsed through Picasso and Thomas Edison pulses through me.

Any one of us can be anything we're bold enough to claim. It's why we see quadriplegics painting beautiful pictures, brushes clenched between their teeth. It's why we see blind people snow-boarding down mountains. The only thing that holds any of us back is ourselves. Opportunities clamor from every side. But many of us are too fainthearted to see the possibilities.

When we refuse to be bold, when we forget to say, "I count," we might as well hand in our keys. Without boldness, life is little but rote recitation.

When Walt Disney was in grade school, a well-meaning teacher, peering over at the flowers he was scribbling in the margins of his paper, tapped him on the shoulder and said, "Walt, honey, those flowers are nice, but flowers don't have faces."

Walt turned around, looked her straight in the eye and pronounced boldly, "Mine do."

This is the boldness with which we must live. We must refuse to listen to anything or anybody except the inner urgings of our soul.

As for Walt Disney, well, his flowers certainly did have faces. In *Alice in Wonderland,* his eighteenth animated feature, the flowers not only had faces, but they had voices, opinions, and a chorus that entertained Alice with the whimsical song, "All in the Golden Afternoon."

People Who Live Big

SAMUEL MOCKBEE
If We Build It, They Will Live

WE HAVE TO CHALLENGE THE STATUS QUO
TO ALLOW FOR A BETTER FUTURE.

—*Samuel Mockbee*

Samuel Mockbee had it made. He owned a successful architecture firm. Many of his designs won prestigious awards. He was taking on projects of an international scale. He had enough free time to paint and pursue other hobbies. But something bigger was calling him.

A fifth-generation Alabaman, he knew firsthand about the long-lingering problems of race and poverty in his state. And while many of us would shrug and say, "Well, it's certainly a crying shame, but what can I really do?" Mockbee took what he could do—design homes—and put it to use.

A professor at Auburn University, Mockbee not only wanted to put his money and his time where his heart was, but he wanted to make sure his first love—architecture—was being used for a noble purpose.

He started the Rural Studio to help his students understand what architecture was really about. He believed people should live in harmony with their environment. He believed architecture could address social values as well as technical and aesthetic values.

The idea for Rural Studio started in 1993, when Mockbee, frustrated by student projects that were built only to be torn down, had a bigger idea. Why not build walls in real homes where people could really use them? Why spend all this time coming up with designs that are only theoretical when we could spend the same amount of time designing things that are useful?

He and his students headed to Hale County, Alabama, one of the poorest counties in America, where a good 36 percent of the population lives below the poverty line.

Surely, they could use some unique housing ideas. What if we could build them homes and try our hand at innovative architecture at the same time? What if we could build these homes ourselves for people who could not otherwise afford them? What if we could offer them for free?

Needless to say, a person has to think out of the box to come up with an idea like that. And, in fact, Mockbee and his students have completely torn open the envelope on what's possible in building homes. Rather than follow old forms that say, "Homes are made of wood, brick, or stone," they came up with innovative designs that used offbeat building materials, such as old tires, hay bales, bottles, and even cast-off license plates.

Suddenly, people who had lived in substandard housing their entire lives had not only warm, safe homes, but homes that Mockbee likes to call "warm, safe homes with spirit." A home, Mockbee says, should be a shelter for the soul as well as the body.

His students do all the work themselves—from the design to the pounding of nails. They literally live for an entire semester in this impoverished county that's an hour from the closest movie theater.

Mockbee says Rural Studio is a far cry from normal college life, where you attend classes with fellow students a couple times a week. At Rural Studio, they live together, cook together, eat together, and create wonderful homes together. The studio is a converted 1890s farmhouse.

Over the years, Mockbee's students have built chapels, basketball courts, and several homes, including a wonderful 850-square-foot home from hay bales. Alberta and Shepard Bryant, proud owners of this new home, were living with three grandkids in a leaky shack with no plumbing until Mockbee and his students showed up.

The students also built a backyard smokehouse out of broken concrete curbing and multicolored glass. Ringing in at a mere $20, the smokehouse where Shepard smokes fish is beautiful, with light coming through the colorful glass. As Mockbee says, "We take something that is very ordinary and make it extraordinary."

His goal? "I want to jump into the dark and see where I land." It is the only way.

People Who Live Big

BRUCE POON TIP

Not Leaving Footprints, but Leaving a Legacy

> I WAS BORN TO BE AN EXPLORER.
> THERE WAS NEVER ANY DECISION TO MAKE.
> I COULDN'T DO ANYTHING ELSE AND BE HAPPY.
>
> —*Roy Chapman Andrews*

Ten years ago, when Bruce Poon Tip decided to start his own adventure travel company, he could have focused on the fact he was only twenty-three years old, a virtual kid in the eyes of most potential customers. Or he could have dwelled on the fact that he'd been fired from the only two jobs he'd ever had— Denny's when he was sixteen and McDonald's a few months later. Or he could have remembered that the last business he tried, a mail order company selling yarn bookmarks that told the weather, was closed down by his school principal because his classmates were skipping school to fill orders.

But instead of "facing facts," this gutsy entrepreneur said, "I know I can," and launched what turned out to be a revolutionary leader in the booming travel industry.

Not only is Poon Tip's Toronto-based G.A.P. Adventures a money-making leader (it pulled down a cool $16 million last year and consistently ranks in Canada's Profit 100, an annual ranking of fastest growing companies), but it lives the socially responsible philosophy it promotes.

"Leaving no footprints," a common mantra for ecotourism operators, is not good enough for G.A.P. Yes, Poon Tip limits his trips to twelve people, relies solely on local transportation—trains, horses, dugout canoes—and insists on staying in small guesthouses and B&Bs, but he also makes sure his "footprints" make a tangible difference in the lives of the people he works with. Thanks to Poon Tip, the Pimpilala Indians, a small tribe in the rainforest of Ecuador, have been able to purchase sacred tribal land. No longer having to rely on logging to survive, the tribe has been able to halt oil and mining exploration that was stripping their lands.

All G.A.P. clients are offered the chance to "adopt" a kid from the country they visit.

And if trips do not follow Poon Tip's environmental, ethical, and social codes, he'll dump them—even if they are successful. A popular gorilla tracking trip to Uganada, one of Poon Tip's best-sellers, was canceled when it became apparent that tour operators he worked with weren't treating guides fairly. Another time, he pulled out of Burma when government officials wouldn't let him work with—and therefore benefit—local people.

Back at the office, Poon Tip also lives his noble views. All seventy-five employees start with four weeks vacation. Each gets a free trip a year. And to follow the low-impact philosophy, each employee gets a free bus pass or is encouraged to walk, copy paper is used on both sides, and Poon Tip pays nearly double for fair market coffee.

Poon Tip's decision to Live Big all started after two mind-opening trips to Thailand.

"The first, an expensive five-star bus tour, led me to believe that Thailand was filled with yuppies and fancy hotels. I went back, and on my own for $5 a day, discovered hill tribes and small villages. I saw the real Thailand. I realized on the first tour

I'd been trapped in a Western environment. I figured others might want the same thing I did," he says.

He was right. The company has grown exponentially in ten years. And while it might be tempting to rest on his laurels, Poon Tip just launched an adventure television series, the pilot following a ten-day trek through Borneo, at the Bampf film festival.

Young, ballsy, and unwilling to fit into ruts, Poon Tip is a visionary, and his mission is nothing short of "saving the world." He's an advisor to the World Bank in Washington, and his ethical beliefs earned him last year's Ethics in Action award.

He knows it's not enough to have big cars and big homes (although he certainly lives life with *joie de vivre*—he flew fifty of his closest friends to Ecuador for his wedding last year at a remote resort, a three-hour boat ride away from Coca, in the middle of the rain forest). What matters to Poon Tip is making a difference, leaving a legacy, making the world a better place.

People Who Live Big

BEV SANDERS
Helping Annie Oakley Sing,
"Anything You Can Do..."

NOT OFTEN IN LIFE WE DO WE GET OPPORTUNITIES TO MAKE A CHANGE AND WE SHOULD THINK OF IT THAT WAY ...AS AN OPPORTUNITY RATHER THAN AN OBSTACLE.

—*Bev Sanders*

When Bev Sanders was in high school, her dad gave her an office job in his driving school. "Forget college," he said. "Girls don't need an education. What will you do with it once you get married?"

Even though she loved her dad and understood that he was only the product of his generation, Bev quite wisely packed her bags and moved west.

She got a job in Lake Tahoe teaching skiing, a passion she'd had since childhood. That bold move, that decision to abandon old ways of thinking and leap into a new possibility, set the stage for an incredibly big life.

Not only did she start one of the first companies to design and manufacture snowboards, but she is doing everything within her power to change the way women see themselves—particularly when it comes to sports.

"Look at the ads. Even today, 99 percent of them show men doing the sports," she says. "Where are the women? My mission is to level the playing field."

Even in her own company, Avalanche Snowboards, a business she co-founded in 1982 with her husband Chris, it was tough getting recognition for "girls'" snowboarding needs. She had a terrible time convincing Chris and other designers to build a performance board for girls. She had to really work to justify the initial $20,000 mold expense. Even avid female snowboarders would say, "Well, this is what my boyfriend says I should try."

"But I felt I had a social responsibility to do what I believed in," she says.

Finally, after much hell-bent determination, Bev convinced Avalanche to come out with the Sanders 148, the first snowboard designed solely for women. Within a year, it won an award for best free-riding board and established a trend for women-specific boards.

"People always say to me, 'You're just one person. How can you affect the world?'" she says. "Well, I believe I can."

She certainly has affected the ski industry. When she and Chris first started designing snowboards on the back of bar napkins, snowboarding was a renegade sport. Most ski resorts wouldn't even allow snowboards on the slopes. Bev and Chris had to put up their dukes just to find a place to "test ride" their products. Today, of course, snowboards are everywhere, and in 1998, sixteen years after Bev first held fast to her belief that snowboards were possible, it became an Olympic sport.

In fact, snowboarding finally became so mainstream that Bev lost interest. She and Chris sold the company in 1995. "When MTV picked it up, I knew it was over for me. Gap might as well have been selling snowboards," she says.

Her current passion is a girls-only surf school that she started on a beach north of Puerto Vallarta, Mexico. Called Las Olas Surf Safaris, the company's mission, says Bev, is to empower women through surfing and snowboarding.

"Women bond in a special way," she says. "I especially love to see these corporate women show up. Within twenty-four hours they're acting like a bunch of monkeys. I always joke that I'm running a reverse finishing school, that I make girls out of women."

The seven-day programs, best described as a cross between a slumber party and an empowerment seminar, incorporate yoga, massage, and daily surf lessons. For Bev, it's a way of helping women claim their power.

"We need strong women. Women are the ones who will stand up for the environment, who will do what needs to be done. We need women's strength to change the world," she says.

After years of snowboarding, Bev discovered her passion for surfing only by being bold. She and Chris had standby airline reservations to Milan. When their plane was sold out, they went to the next counter, and a flight that happened to be going to Maui.

"We didn't even have swimsuits or shorts. We checked into a hotel, I picked up the phone book and saw an ad in the yellow pages with a dog on a surfboard. It said, 'If a dog can surf, so can you.' We went and got the boards and didn't bring them back until seven days later. It changed my life," she says.

"I feel so privileged as a human being to be at the beginning of two different things: first snowboarding and now bringing more women into sports," she says.

Thinking Bold

THE TIME WE LIVE IN
REQUIRES A NEW WAY OF THINKING.

—*Albert Einstein*

Who, when you really think about it, wants to do unimportant and uninteresting things? Yet, look how we spend our time. Look at the headlines in the magazines we read. Look at the TV shows we're addicted to.

We think we care about things that we really don't. I hate to be the one to break it to you, but you really don't care what perfume you're wearing, whether or not you've mastered the secrets of the sixty-minute orgasm.

You care about what happens to our children. To our oceans. To the big beautiful American dream of freedom and equality and unlimited possibilities. You care about your soul, about God, about how you can make a difference in the world.

Somehow, we've gotten off track. I don't really know how it happened. I'm not even sure we need to know. Figuring out why we've gotten off track is another of those irrelevant issues that we spend way too much time on. It doesn't matter.

The only thing that matters now is "How can we get back on track?" How can take our focus off trivial and unimportant things and put it back where it belongs?

When we focus on insignificant issues, we deny our true selves. This is a big problem, folks. It's why Eli Lilly has made a fortune on Prozac. It's why forty people will try to kill themselves in the next hour.

We are gods playing fools. We are pretending to care about things we don't care about. It doesn't matter how much money you make, what kind of car you drive. You don't care. It's like we're all playing make-believe, only somehow we forgot that it's make-believe.

The only thing that you really care about is how you can boldly make a difference in this world, how you can best spread love to your brothers and sisters. All of us recognize this truth—whether we admit it or not. It's the still, small voice that continually pokes us in the ribs, the discontent that flows through us when we stop long enough to think, "Is this all there is?"

The still small voice will never shut up. It's like the energizer bunny. Or a dandelion. You just can't get rid of it. So why don't we all just put down our arms, call, "Ally-ally, oxen all in free," and admit it.

We all really love each other. We all long to do big things. We can save our world. It's not too late.

3 Big ?s

I ALWAYS SAY TO MYSELF, WHAT IS THE
MOST IMPORTANT THING WE CAN THINK ABOUT
IN THIS EXTRAORDINARY MOMENT.

—*R. Buckminster Fuller*

Before Native American people make important decisions, they ask themselves, "How will this decision affect my children and the seven generations to follow?" When the rest of us make important decisions, we mostly want to know how it will affect our bank statement. Maybe instead, we should be asking ourselves:

1.

What would I do if I knew I couldn't fail?

2.

How can I step outside that little line that society prescribes as "normal"?

3.

What one thing can I do today to bring brilliance and wonder into my awareness?

Boot Camp for the Soul

Make a Fool of Yourself
at Least Once Every Day

A MAN NEEDS A LITTLE MADNESS, OR ELSE HE NEVER
DARES CUT THE ROPE AND BE FREE.

—*Nikos Kazantzakis*

Assignment: Each day for seven days, do something that you have *never* done before and something you feel that you simply *cannot* do.

How many times have you had a good idea only to keep it to yourself for fear of looking like a crackpot? How many times have you wanted to run up and hug someone and tell them how much you love them, but you didn't because, well, they might not feel the same? Or they might think you're one of those loony bins "they" warned them about.

Well, this fear of appealing foolish is crippling. Worrying what other people think squelches our joy, our fun, and all those good ideas our planet needs.

The prescription for overcoming this "debilitating disease" is to force yourself to do absurd things. Ingrid Torrance, an actress who appeared in the film, *Double Jeopardy* with Ashley Judd, says, "I had a huge lack of confidence. I faced my fear of acting by doing things that made me uncomfortable."

C. W. Metcalf, a humor consultant to many Fortune 500 companies, says he cured himself of "terminal seriousness" by forcing himself to do things like walk through an airport minus a sock and shoe. Or stand in an elevator and talk nonstop.

Notice your reaction. Do you find yourself thinking?, "I could never in a million years do that!" Be assured that this resistance is the same thing that's keeping you stuck.

Your assignment is to do one absurd thing every day for seven days. One thing that you are sure "you could never do." Yes, it has to be in public. And, yes, it has to be something out of the ordinary, something that might make people laugh.

But, but . . . what if people DO laugh?

Take a bow. As Dr. Thomas Sydenham, a seventeenth-century physician, said, "The arrival of a good clown exercises more beneficial influence upon the health of a town than 20 asses laden with drugs."

People love to laugh. They need to laugh. According to Patch Adams, "People crave laughter like an essential amino acid." And since everybody else on this planet is just as eager to break out of their ruts as you are, people will love your crazy stunts.

If anything, they'll be jealous, wish it were them.

But I guarantee you they won't forsake you. You might even inspire them. People are desperately longing for someone to give them permission to be themselves. You can be the one who gives them that permission.

And if your mind is so stuck that you can't even think of any ideas, try a couple of these ideas:

⑥ *Hang out on elevators.* If there's one place where acceptable behavior is rigidly prescribed, it's on an elevator. People would rather slit their veins in a warm bath than talk to each other. In fact, they stand there like deaf mutes looking intently at the ceiling or their shoes. It's the perfect place to begin your pilgrimage.

⑥ *Ditch the dress code.* Clown costumes are good. A Richard

Nixon mask would work. Given the narrowness of fashion standards today, it's not too difficult to come up with something that will make people chuckle, point, and realize that maybe there are other possibilities.

Wear your new get-up to the library, to the dry cleaners, yes, even to work. You'll be surprised at how much fun you'll have.

As Patch says, "Wearing underwear on the outside of your clothes can turn a tedious trip to the store for a forgotten carton of milk into an amusement park romp."

Of course, Patch also owns a gorilla costume. And a ballet tutu. And for someone who is 6 feet 6 inches with hair down to his waist, that's not a look likely to show up on the cover of *Vanity Fair.*

Patch's ridiculous raiment, as he calls these outrageous outfits, reminds us that we often live in other people's ruts, that we do most things without thinking. Because we think we have to. Or because we're conditioned that way. It doesn't even cross our mind that we could try something else.

⊚ *Try outlandish, even ridiculous things.* Patch, for example, hosted a fund-raiser in Phoenix called "Full Moon over Camelback" where thousands of people paid $25 for the privilege of mooning the city in unison at the stroke of midnight. As charity events go, it was pure genius—no overhead, no auctions, no selling things nobody really wants.

CHAPTER 2

Giving Big:
The Attitude
of Service

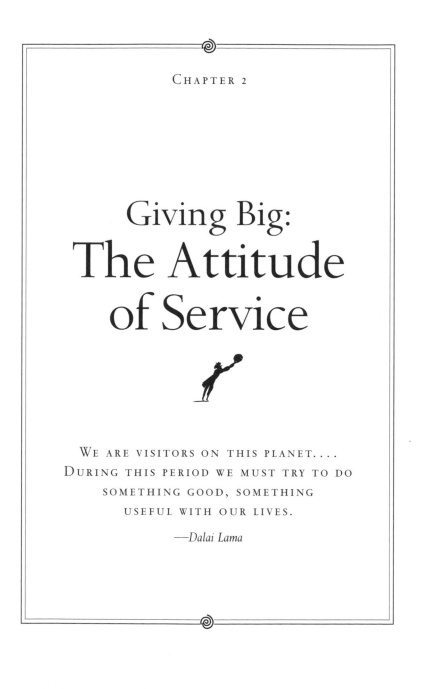

WE ARE VISITORS ON THIS PLANET....
DURING THIS PERIOD WE MUST TRY TO DO
SOMETHING GOOD, SOMETHING
USEFUL WITH OUR LIVES.

—*Dalai Lama*

espite what Madison Avenue would like us to believe, that vacation to the Riviera, that Chrysler PT Cruiser, that anti-aging cream is not the secret to happiness. There's only one thing that unlocks the door to true peace of mind. Serving a purpose bigger than that face you see in the mirror every morning. Giving everything you've got to making your world a better, brighter, more beautiful place.

Most of us haven't a clue how to give. We operate on a clandestine barter system. You do this and then I'll do that. You scratch my back; I'll scratch yours. Admit it or not, we all give for what we think we might get back. It's not always money. Many of us seek appreciation or love or that pearl necklace from Tiffany's. But as long as we keep a scorecard tally, we're destined to be stuck in the same old quagmire of fear.

When you go through life expecting people to do things for you, even if it's only seeing things the way you do, you're playing victim. You're taking from the world, not giving.

Giving Big means ditching the victim schtick.

"But I'm not a victim!" you protest. Anytime you deny your own responsibility in any situation, you're playing victim. If you've ever believed that some person, some circumstance, some outer reason caused you to do anything, you've played victim.

Try these statements on for size.

"I can't help it. It's just the way I am."
"Well, you see, I had this terrible childhood."
"I'm sick and tired of _____."
"Why does this always happen to me?"
"My life will never be the same."
"The world is getting so crazy these days."
"People are so insensitive."

See what I mean! You need to "grow up and get over yourself."

When we really become big enough to serve, to give it all away with no expectation, our sense of personal power, our peace of mind, and our ability to love and trust takes giant steps.

Albert Schweitzer is the perfect example. He was a renowned organist, an author, an expert on Bach. But when he read about the atrocious health conditions in Africa, he could no longer "live for himself."

He put himself through medical school, defied family and friends who thought he was crazy to leave his prosperous career and go to the jungles of Africa. "You're being unreasonable," they said. "You should stay in Europe. You can raise money for medical care here."

But as he said, "We must not ask whether a goal is reasonable. We must act according to our own inner compulsion."

His own inner compulsion said, "Go!" He started the Lambarene Medical Center in the only building he could find—

a chicken coop. Within nine months, he had treated 2,000 patients. For the next fifty years, he worked in the jungles of Africa, saving lives, inspiring millions.

Even when he won the Nobel Peace Prize in 1953, he used the $33,000 award to start a nearby leper colony. He said repeatedly that as long as there was even one man who was hungry, sick, lonely, or living in fear, that man was his responsibility.

"Everyone," he said, "must find his own Lambarene."

People Who Live Big

MARY GUTHRIE

Her Crazy Love Works Big Miracles

I HATE RULES. I'M THE WORLD'S
CRAPPIEST RULE FOLLOWER.

—*Mary Guthrie*

If anyone had reason to feel sorry for herself it was Mary Guthrie. In high school, she jokes, she was voted "most likely to end up in reform school." She eloped with her high school sweetheart when she was only sixteen. Her second child died of SIDS when he was only two months old. The son's untimely death plunged her young husband into a deep depression; he became unable to hold down a job and could usually be found lying on the child's grave crying.

He often took out his pain by beating Mary. To this day she bears a huge scar across her left arm where he cut her in a fit of rage.

Two days after their third child, a second beautiful daughter, was born, he grabbed the new baby by her legs and slammed her against a wall, causing a hearing disorder that requires her to wear hearing aids.

Even though she had a not-quite-week-old baby and a two-year-old, Mary left and never looked back.

When Mickey, the new baby, was four weeks old, Mary went to work at a discount store, doing anything she could to scratch out a living.

In a year, she met and married again. Although her second husband owned a successful construction company, he, too, beat her and eventually plummeted so far into drugs that he was arrested and put on trial in Louisiana.

"My life back then was like a Hollywood set where everything looks beautiful on the outside," she says, "but behind the set it's all held up with sticks."

To top it all off, her fourth child, Allen, now twenty-six, was born with undiagnosed developmental delays and seizure disorder. She was advised by "experts" that he'd be better off institutionalized.

At the time he was born, she was twenty-four and already had a six-year-old and a two-year-old. She had no resources, no insurance. Most people might have thought it prudent for Mary to *seek* help.

And for awhile, she did. When Allen was fifteen months old, she put him in a program for special needs kids.

"But it wasn't right for him," she says, and pulled him out six months later.

Paying for everything out of her own pocket, she began taking him to occupational therapists, physical therapists, even to karate lessons. She wouldn't stop until he could ride a trike and then a bike. Today, he drives.

And finally on April 20, 1990, when she reached the ripe old age of forty, she mustered the courage to say "Bye-bye" to her abusive husband and follow her heart. She longed to share what she'd learned about raising kids with special needs.

"I call that day my independence day," she say. "I used to rationalize not leaving him with the thought, 'I have two kids. Who's going to want me?' Then finally one day I said, 'Well, I want me.'"

So what if she was a housewife with no education? So what if she didn't have an official degree or a single credential in special education? So what if she didn't have a trust fund to buy expensive monitors and oxygen equipment?

She decided to take what she did have—the willingness and open-heartedness to see that behind every kid that doctors write off as "hopeless" is a human spirit with unlimited possibilities—and use it to serve.

Despite the fact that life has thrown her some pretty wacky curveballs, she chooses to give, to make a genuine difference in the lives of the thirty-five kids who come to her unconventional special needs program in Lee's Summit, Missouri. Called Giant Step, the center is run by Mary, daughter Mickey, who overcame her deafness and is now a nurse, and son Allen, who serves as transportation director.

"My business card says I'm program director, but what I really am is a mom who had no access to anything in 1973," Guthrie says. "I believe you can make anything your expertise if you want it bad enough."

A veritable clearinghouse of information about special needs, Mary finds that her phone rarely stops ringing. She can reel off the phone numbers for the Spina Bifida Association, the Down's Syndrome Association, and on and on. She coached Special Olympics for nine years. "They called me the other day to ask if I'd coach Special Olympics again this year. I said I'd be glad to if we could practice between 3 and 4:30 A.M., the only time I'm not already booked," says Mary, who for years wore a platinum flattop.

A cross between Erin Brockovich, George Carlin, and Mother Teresa, she'll still try anything to uplift her kids, who suffer with everything from Down's syndrome and autism to seizures and Prader-Willi disease. "My idea is to just get everybody familiar with everybody else. Inside, we're all the same, we just want to be loved and accepted."

Whether it's making a King Tut Halloween costume for a Down's syndrome baby or singing her own personal rendition of "Smoke on the Water" to a kid who can't speak, she's always looking for new ways to reach her kids. She jokes with them and gives them nicknames, a refreshing change in the oh-so-serious world of special needs.

"My motto is 'It's not how long you live. It's how much fun you have,'" she says.

She started Giant Step with Nicholas, a baby whom doctors said would be lucky to live three days. Today, Nicholas is seven, in school and defying all the odds.

When the list of children grew, when Nicholas was joined by Lauren and Jacob and Jenner and Tommy and countless others, Guthrie gave up her home. She just up and moved out, giving it away rent-free so the center could serve more children.

"If you look at the books, we really shouldn't have made it," she says. "It's a miracle we're here at all. Somebody must really want me to do this."

And, no, Giant Step isn't the biggest, most fancy facility you'll ever find ("To my way of thinking, Abe Lincoln was born in a log cabin," Mary says) and between red tape and government regulations, she's always struggling with some problem. "What works in your real world doesn't always work in my real world," she says.

But when you commit yourself to following your dreams, all sorts of doors mysteriously open. Mary, for example, fell—literally stumbled—into freelance writing. Although most people know that "it's impossible" to sell scripts to big network shows, especially if you're forty and live in Nowheresville, Missouri, she approached her new goal the same way she approaches everything in life. "Most people see stone walls. I see a stone wall and immediately start looking where I could pole-vault over," she says.

The money she made selling scripts to such TV series as *Roseanne, In Living Color,* and *Murphy Brown* was the money that funded Giant Step.

Writing for *Roseanne* was an act of total serendipity. In fact, it all started as a crazy dare. Her daughters were visiting, and while watching an episode of the popular sitcom, Mary began ranting about the ending.

A comedienne at heart and a born joketeller, Mary said, "I could come up with a better line than that. They could have gotten three more laughs."

"OK, big shot," her daughters said to her. "If you're so funny, why don't you write an episode?"

That night, she sat down with a spiral notebook (she didn't even own a typewriter, and proper script format—what is that?) and began writing an episode. Fourteen hours later, she had a complete script.

"Did I think I'd be a writer? I was always funny, the life of the PTA, but I'd never entertained the notion of writing professionally. In fact, my famous writer story was the 10,000-word theme one of the Catholic sisters asked me to write over the weekend in high school. The subject was 'How I Can Be a Better Catholic' and it was punishment for something I'd done." For the assignment, she had her brother take ten Polaroids of her in various vestibules and pews of the church and pasted them together with "A picture is worth a thousand words."

Eventually, she did learn about proper script format and did have success selling to all the shows she wanted to write for.

"But my heart was, is and always will be with the children," she explains. Even when she had a mild stroke and was being rushed to the hospital, she was wondering how one of her moms' mediation went, she was checking with Mickey to make sure Lauren, one of the other Down's syndrome babies, had the pennies in her socks for what Mary called "weight training."

Nothing stops Mary Guthrie. She overcame ovarian cancer in 1991. She's currently battling a lung problem that she developed from the mold in the many rehab projects she takes on.

"People always ask me, 'How do you do it? How do you learn about all these disabilities?'" she says. "And I tell them, 'You learn about them one at a time. You learn to love the kids one at a time. You try different tricks one at a time.'"

Today, at fifty, Guthrie is probably the happiest, most empowered person I know. She doesn't make big bucks. In fact, she's quite proud of the fact that she can live on less than

$20,000 a year. She knows with a quiet certainty that life isn't about what you can get. But how much you can give.

Instead of bemoaning her fate in life, grumbling about the bad luck of losing a child or having two who were disabled, she took what she did have—a huge heart, a wry sense of humor and a whole lot of experience working with her own special needs kids—and turned her life into something extraordinary.

Mary Guthrie knows who she is. She knows she has big things to do, that her life makes a difference. And she found it all by giving big.

People Who Live Big

JAMES TWYMAN

Singing Songs and Praying for World Peace

THIS IS THE TIME WE'VE BEEN WAITING FOR.
WE'RE READY.

—*James Twyman*

Raised as a devout Irish Catholic, James Twyman has always felt a deep connection with the Divine. He talked his priest into letting him be an altar boy before he was actually old enough. He entered the Franciscan priesthood the minute he finished high school.

But after two years, he got disillusioned and decided to re-enter secular life. He went to college, married, had a daughter, sold Craft-o-matic beds. Like many people in the secular life,

Twyman felt dissatisfied. His marriage didn't work out. He went through a five- or six-year dark night of the soul.

Finally, he landed in southside Chicago at St. Catherine's Catholic Worker, a residence for people who were both homeless and living with AIDS. There, working with people in need, he says, "I finally quit thinking about myself."

That was the turning point in his life, the attitude shift that turned his life into a big one.

As a kid, he had longed to be a rock star. As early as twelve, he learned to play the guitar, honing his skills while playing and singing songs for family and friends.

While working at St. Catherine's, someone serendipitously passed along a collection of prayers from the twelve major religions. "I noticed they all had the same goal," he says. "The universal theme was peace within."

Almost immediately upon reading the prayers, music began dancing through Twyman's head. Rather than deny the still, small voice, he sat down and wrote out guitar music to each of the twelve peace prayers.

From that point on, Twyman knew exactly what he wanted to do. He would be a traveling mendicant peace troubadour. He would sing his peace songs to whoever would listen. He would share his music wherever there was violence in the world. He would organize prayers for peace. He would plant peace poles in areas of conflict.

"There's a power in music that cannot be found in many other places. I felt that maybe people could hear through music and prayer what they were not hearing through the politicians—that it was time to turn toward peace," he said. "I decided to go to those places where peace was needed the most."

But ... but ... who gave him permission? What organization does he work for? When you find your passion, the last thing you need is permission. And if there's not an organization doing what you feel led to do, you create your own.

In February 1998, while being interviewed on a British radio show and not thinking anyone would take him seriously, he made a silly comment that he'd like to sing the Muslim peace prayer to Saddam Hussein. At the time, war with Iraq seemed imminent. A British ambassador to Iraq just happened to hear the interview and within two days, Twyman was on a plane heading for Tehran. He gave a nationally televised peace concert and sent out an e-mail inviting people to send the feeling of peace as he performed. Millions of people from around the world responded. Three days later, a peace accord was signed.

The following week, James was invited to Northern Ireland, where the peace talks in Belfast were stalled. Again, he sang and again, he put out an e-mail asking for prayers to be focused on Northern Ireland. Three days later, a breakthrough occurred in the talks that allowed the peace accord to be signed a month ahead of schedule.

On November 13, 1998, nine months after the Iraqui Peace Concert, newspaper headlines declared that negotiations with Hussein had broken off. The United States was about to attack at any moment. James, along with a couple of other authors and big thinkers, organized another Internet prayer campaign.

"Little did we know," James says, "that on the same day we were holding the worldwide prayer vigil, President Clinton had given the order to attack. Planes were in the air waiting for orders to begin bombing. Within hours of the vigil, Clinton gave an unprecedented stand down order, calling the planes back, not once, but twice. As far as I know, this has never occurred with an executive order."

Although there is no sure method for scientifically measuring the connection between millions of prayers for world peace and the signing of peace treaties, there certainly appears to be a correlation.

In 2000, Yassir Arafat made the comment that it would take a million prayers before peace would ever come to the Middle East. So Twyman did what any good peace troubadour would do. He began a massive Internet campaign to collect those one million prayers. And when he gets them all, he plans to head to the Middle East and personally present them to Mr. Arafat.

Just one person? Making a huge difference.

According to Twyman, the message of peace boils down to a simple, three-word question:

Are you ready?

Yes, I'm ready.

People Who Live Big

SUSAN KRABACHER

From the Playboy Mansion to the Slums of Haiti

I CAN STOP THEIR TEARS IN A SECOND JUST
BY WALKING UP. YOU CAN'T BUY THAT.

—*Susan Krabacher*

To look on the outside, Susan Krabacher was living mighty big. Blonde, beautiful, married to a wealthy Aspen businessman, she had everything most of us long for. She'd modeled for sixteen years, been a *Playboy* cover girl, lived in the same ritzy neighborhood as Kevin Costner.

But in October 1994, while contemplating whether or not to open a second antique store, she happened to watch a TV special about poverty in Mongolia. She said to her husband, "Boy, I'd like to do something to help those people." She wrote to several charities, and while they there more than happy to take her money, none of them wanted her "hands-on" help. They said she wasn't qualified, had no training.

"Fine," she said. "I'll do it myself."

Richard Dusseau, a management consultant friend from her church, suggested she accompany him to Haiti. "It's ten times as poor and it's right in our own hemisphere," he said.

Within a month, Susan was on a plane. Within a week of arriving in Haiti, she had thrown away her passport. And within seven years, her Foundation for Worldwide Mercy and Sharing funds five orphanages, six schools, and two medical clinics, helping as many as 1,600 abandoned kids a year.

"I can never imagine myself without them," she says.

And while Susan did get her passport back and still maintains a residence in Aspen, she spends four to six months a year in Haiti, singing to babies—some of whom die in her arms—hugging kids stuck by bed sores to their mattresses, and feeding hundreds of kids whose main sustenance is scraps they can scrounge from the knee-deep garbage pile they live on.

For her trouble, she's contracted lice, scabies, mange, and encephalitis. She's battled gangs who have stolen her equipment and held guns to her head, she's contended with hurricanes, and she's defied government officials who wanted bribes for letting her care for the children.

"They wanted $300 for every child. That's more than two years salary in Haiti," she said. "I told them, 'Fine, I'll have the kids back in the morning.' I never heard from them again."

Dusseau was certainly right about the poverty. Haiti is widely recognized as the poorest country in the Western Hemisphere. Seventy percent of the population is unemployed. Those lucky enough to work make an average of $150 a year. Homes are so small that family members take turns sleeping.

On her first trip there, Susan, who was used to glamorous digs in Aspen, insisted on spending the night in Cite Soleil, a twenty-seven-square-mile slum where nearly a million people live. She shared a one-room shanty with seventeen Haitians.

"I could hardly hug her the next day, she smelled so bad," Dusseau says.

Even when she lived in Hugh Hefner's Los Angeles mansion, Susan had a heart for needy kids, forged no doubt by her own rough childhood. Molested by a grandfather at age eight and sent to foster care when she was twelve, she knows what it's like to be poor. Although she was rejoined with her own family when she was fourteen, she was disowned again at seventeen after a photographer sent photos of her in a bikini to the *Playboy* magnate.

Claiming to be older than she was, Susan was driven from her Utah home by a limousine to the Los Angeles mansion. "I hid for three days," she says. "I was terrified, afraid I'd see orgies." Finally, she did make friends with the other models and joined in the nightly circus at Hef's place, where she lived on and off for about a year.

Despite the fun, the money, and the notoriety (she was a *Playboy* centerfold in 1983), Susan suffered low self-esteem and contracted anorexia. In 1984 a short-lived marriage took her to

Aspen, where she met Joe, her present husband, an attorney who handled her divorce.

Although the marriage to Joe was a success and she enjoyed her antique business, she didn't really find her true mission until she traveled to Haiti and saw 100 little cribs with dying children in the abandoned children's ward at Port-au-Prince's government hospital.

"I thought she would go down, write a check, hold a few babies, and hit the road," says the friend who invited her to Haiti. "I had no idea she go at it with such a vengeance."

"I didn't want the epitaph on my gravestone to read, 'She was Miss May 1983,'" Susan says.

Small Ways to Be Big

WE MAKE A LIVING BY WHAT WE GET;
WE MAKE A LIFE BY WHAT WE GIVE.

—*Winston Churchill*

With all the problems in the world, finding your niche can seem overwhelming. I mean, how can I, one person, solve world hunger? How can I, a single mom, solve the AIDS epidemic? Well, I can't. But I can bake a cookie for a starving homeless kid. And I can massage the back of the artist in my neighborhood who has AIDS. And each time, I make these seemingly tiny contributions, the world becomes a tiny bit sweeter, a tiny bit closer to heaven.

Not all of us are Jonas Salk. But we make a huge mistake if we believe our gifts and our contributions, no matter how small, don't count. Diane Heinen gets up 365 days a year—rain, sleet, or snow—to drive to the gas station on the main drag of her hometown of Valley Falls, Kansas (pop. 1,200). Using white shoe polish, she writes "Happy Birthday" in large block letters to everyone having a birthday that day. She has a list with every resident's birthday, and she even remembers former Valley Falls' residents—even if they now live in Timbuktu.

Small thing? Not if you ask residents of Valley Falls, who have an incredible community spirit.

Last Valentine's Day, my friend, Kitty, was without a job. Her mortgage was due the next day. She wasn't sure how she was going to feed Grace and Maggie, her two dogs, let alone how she was going to come up with a $1,000 mortgage payment.

"They say" would surely have insisted it prudent to spend the day sending out resumes.

But Kitty decided to defy "they say." She spent her last $15 on Valentine's cards and kids' party favors. She addressed each valentine "To My Friend" and signed them "From Your Friend."

She put red ribbons around Maggie's and Grace's necks, stuck them in her Mazda Miata, and headed out. She passed out Valentines, each with a plastic airplane or a bracelet, to forty children, many who were in the hospital with tubes sticking out of their hearts.

She'd walk into a hospital room and say, "I've been looking for you all day."

At first, the parents looked at each other with a look of bemusement. "Who is this weird person?" they'd think.

But the kids knew.

According to Kitty, it was the best Valentine's Day she'd ever had. Yes, "they say" she should have been pining away for the boyfriend she didn't have or the job that was slow in coming. But by taking her "blocks" of humor and love, she was reminded of what a big person she is and always has been.

Serving humanity can take many forms, but it always involves spreading love, building people up, making children smile. Ultimately, it's the only thing that will ever make you happy.

3 Big ?s

COMPARED WITH WHAT WE OUGHT TO BE,
WE ARE ONLY HALF AWAKE. OUR FIRES ARE
DAMPED, OUR DRAFTS ARE CHECKED.
WE ARE MAKING USE OF ONLY A SMALL
PART OF OUR POSSIBLE MENTAL
AND PHYSICAL RESOURCES.

—*William James*

In a recent poll, 21 percent of North Americans reported that they were regularly "bored out of their minds." Been there, done that, so what? But as Helen Keller once said, "No pessimist ever discovered the secrets of the stars, or sailed to an uncharted land or opened a new Heaven to the human spirit." Ask yourself, "How can I open a new heaven to the human spirit?" along with:

1.

What does my life stand for?

2.

How would I live my life if I were the only person on the planet?

3.

What one thing do I do better than anyone else?
How can I share that with others?

Boot Camp for the Soul

Secret Service Man!

IF WE ALL DID THE THINGS WE ARE CAPABLE OF
DOING, WE WOULD LITERALLY ASTOUND OURSELVES.

—*Thomas Edison*

Assignment: For the next seven days, practice what the Constructive Living folks call "secret service."

We've looked just about everywhere—the want ads, personal growth seminars, the psychiatrist's couch—and still we're wondering what the meaning of life is.

We're still, after twenty years of searching, unclear about our purpose. We thought it might be that great career, that exciting penthouse overlooking the harbor, but, alas, when we finally clawed our way there, that derned hole was still there, still begging to be filled.

Finding out who you are and why you are here involves service to your fellow humans. There is no other way. That service can take many forms, but it always involves spreading love, building people up, making children smile.

For the next seven days, try secret service, a common assignment for folks who practice Constructive Living, an action-based way of looking at the world that eschews Western psychotherapy's tendency to overanalyze our backgrounds and feelings and just get on with it.

Secret service, however small or large, must be performed without anyone else being aware of it. Maybe you could mow your neighbor's lawn while she's away at work. Or leave cookies on the doorstep of a shut-in. Remember, no one is supposed to know it was you. It takes away that need we all have to get brownie points, to get ego strokes.

Serving in a quiet, simple way is a natural inclination of the soul, a natural inclination that many of us have forgotten.

And while, yes, it helps other people, the real reason that we serve our brothers and sisters is that it reminds us of a bigger reality, it keeps us positioned on the fact that we are much more than our neuroses or our little ways. When you finally learn to serve big, to give it all away, you quickly realize that you're much more than a number, much more than a small speck in a huge, cold world.

A Dozen Little Things You Can Do Today to Brighten the World

1.

Pick up a piece of trash. Just one small piece. If everyone picked up one pop can, one candy wrapper, one small something that somebody accidentally left behind, we could clean up our world.

2.

Send a postcard with ten words to someone you love. All you need is an address and something simple like: "Just wanted you to know I absolutely adore you." Imagine what that could do for someone's day.

3.

While you're buying postcards, get one for a childhood hero (a teacher, perhaps, or the next door neighbor who always stopped at your lemonade stand) and send them twenty words letting them know they made a difference in your life. Something like: "Was just remembering how much I always appreciated those chocolate chip cookies you used to invite me over for."

4.

Get a roll of pennies (50 cents—what a bargain) and leave them around a grade school playground.

5.

*Find the manager in a store you frequent and let
her know what a great job one of the employees is doing.*

6.

*Take a flower or a hot cinnamon roll to the
guy who works by himself at the convenience store.*

7.

Laugh spontaneously in public at least three times.

8.

Leave a cheerful "Good morning" on the mirror with lipstick.

9.

Give out three compliments before lunch.

10.

Chalk a poem on a park sidewalk.

11.

Learn three little-known facts about Martin Luther King, Jr.

12.

*Invite all your friends to watch the sunset.
Hold up cards (numbered 1 to 10) to rate the show.*

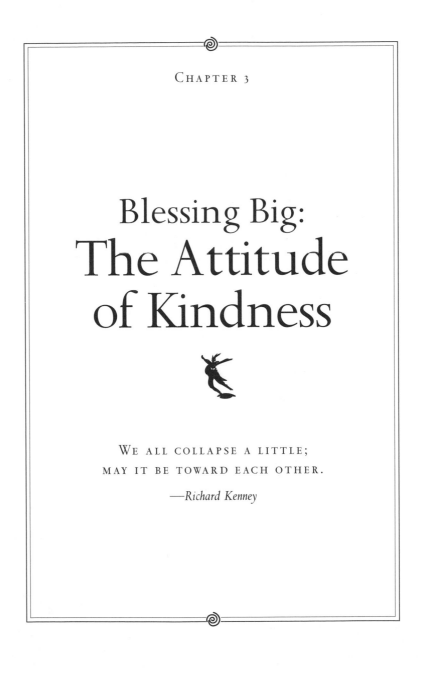

CHAPTER 3

Blessing Big: The Attitude of Kindness

WE ALL COLLAPSE A LITTLE;
MAY IT BE TOWARD EACH OTHER.

—*Richard Kenney*

here are some who might argue that in our world of global pollution, racial cleansing, and famine, kindness is a "soft issue," a luxury we can afford to discuss *after* the problems have been addressed. But until we practice kindness, all our grand schemes and political posturing will be in vain.

The world's a sadder place today. Old men sleep in refrigerator boxes. Ten-year-olds have track lines. Executives with power suits and cell phones don't notice either of them. How could they, in their Land Rovers with tinted glass windows?

The rest of us shrug. Every day, it seems we grow further and further apart. But it doesn't have to be that way.

By practicing kindness, by sticking out a hand, or by offering a thumb's-up to our brothers and sisters, we can alter the world. By smiling at strangers, by going out of our way to applaud each other, we can bind the world back together.

Leaving flowers under a stranger's windshield or quarters in the schoolyard sandbox may seem like a small thing, but the reverberations they create are immense.

Lots of people pooh-poohed the movie *Pay It Forward,* about an eleven-year-old kid whose teacher challenged him to think of an idea that could change the world. Trevor's idea to do favors for three people who would "pay it forward" by doing favors for three more people was "simplistic, unrealistic, too Hollywood," critics said.

But once again, I have to disagree with what "they say." There was nothing simplistic or small about Trevor's idea. Kindness is a revolutionary act, a radical solution, and it powerfully changed Trevor's world. Even when the junkie ended up back in jail, even when the elderly woman died, even when he'd given up on his own plan, Trevor's acts of kindness had borne unexpected fruit. This troubled, latchkey kid had started a movement in which people loved each other, protected each other, and watched over each other. It could go on forever, an unending chain of kindness and generosity.

Kindness is so simple. Yet so profound.

One of my daughter's favorite books, *Somebody Loves You, Mr. Hatch,* is about this lonely little man who gets up every morning at 6:30 to walk eight blocks to the shoelace factory where he works. At lunchtime, he sits alone in a corner, drinking coffee and munching on a cheese and mustard sandwich. After work, he stops to get a paper and a fresh turkey wing. After supper, he reads his paper and goes to bed early so he can get up and start all over again.

One Saturday, the postman brings him a package, a box of candy with a little white card. Inside it says, "Somebody loves you."

Mr. Hatch is shocked. As he dusts his house, he keeps going back to look—is it still there? Does somebody really love me? Who could it be?

Finally, he puts on a yellow tie with blue polka dots, splashes on some aftershave, and goes out for a walk. He waves "Hello" to everyone, a change that makes the neighbors fall off their ladders and trip over their dogs.

At work the next Monday, he goes to the cafeteria and shares his box of chocolates. After work, he offers to watch the newspaper stand so the owner can go to a doctor's appointment. Instead of reading the paper after supper, he bakes brownies and shares them with his neighbors. He even dusts off an old harmonica and plays some tunes he knew as a boy.

This new air of festivity went on for a few weeks until the postman comes back to his home with a sheepish look.

"Ah, do you remember that package I brought you on Valentine's Day?" he stutters.

"Yes," says Mr. Hatch, haltingly.

"I'm afraid I delivered it to the wrong address, and if I don't redeliver, my boss is going to have my job," the postman stammers.

Mr. Hatch gives the postman back the box, although the candy is long gone, consumed by Mr. Hatch's new friends. Suddenly, he realizes, "I don't have a secret admirer, after all." He goes back to his old shirt, his old habit of eating cheese and mustard sandwiches alone in the corner. He neglects to talk to the butcher and the newspaper man.

Everyone starts to wonder, "What's gotten into Mr. Hatch?"

The postman tells them, and they all show up one morning with a big sign that says, "Everybody loves you, Mr. Hatch."

He cries a tear of joy and steps back off the porch to be with his friends.

What a difference one little act of love made in Mr. Hatch's life. One tiny box of chocolate, one three-word card. *Somebody loves you.*

There are thousands of Mr. Hatches out there, and they're just waiting for three little words.

Soul Talk

In northern Russia, they have an expression, "soul talk." It means speaking from the heart, talking about BIG things. Grandparents sit their grandkids under the old oak tree and say, "Let's talk about some big ideas. Let's talk about our souls, about what's important." These conversations can take hours.

In our country, there's not even a word for "soul talk." Parents are too busy following their Day-Timers to sit down and tell their kids, "You know, this is what I believe in. This is where you come from. This is what your grandma did when she was your age. This was what she hoped for you."

According to an article in the *New York Times,* the average parent engages his or her kids in conversation for an average of ten minutes a day. Even stay-at-home moms spend little more than fifteen minutes talking with their children.

By the time you throw in a few "Are you sure your room is picked up?" and a "Did you do your math homework?" there's barely a minute left over for a quick peck or an "I love you."

And what does that really mean? "I love you." Do we sit down with our children and tell them about love? Or do we let them make their own assumptions from the messages they get on the silver screen, the ones where handsome, well-built men look into the eyes of gorgeous beauty queens, coo endearments, and instantaneously find love. Instead of just mouthing the words, maybe we should sit down and tell our kids what love means. That love is when the beauty queen is giving birth to the handsome hunk's babies and he's there holding her hand. Or when he comes home late and she decides to trust him anyway.

We need to spend hours talking about things like love. About big ideas. Big dreams. Not just, "How'd you do on the spelling test?" or, "Okay, who took the remote?" But conversation about deepest hopes, failures, politics, God, bodies, girls, favorite type of Jell-O.

Children need hours and hours of conversation with people who are willing to serve as role models. They desperately need a glimpse into the untrampled countryside of their mentors' minds.

Your kids need to talk to you, to hear what you think, and to know who you are. They need to know what you stand for? They need to hear you say that a big idea is far better than a big car, that a big dream is more important than a leather jacket.

Maybe that's why H. Jackson Brown's *Life's Little Instruction Book* was such a hit. Originally a typewritten gift to his son who was leaving for college, the 511 reminders for how to live a happy and rewarding life were eventually published and sold millions of copies.

In essence, Brown was having a "soul talk" with his son. He was saying, "I value you enough to share with you what I think." When he advised his son to "judge a neighborhood by its kindness instead of its property values," "to sing in the shower," "to never skimp on power tools," "to read *Leadership Is an Art* by Max Depree," he was saying, "Here's what I know and what I believe."

Our children need this kind of soul talk.

Anybody who saw *Bull Durham* has to remember Kevin Costner's speech to Susan Sarandon, the four-minute litany about believing in "the soul, the small of a woman's back, the hanging curveball, high fiber, good Scotch, that the novels of Susan Sontag are self-indulgent, overrated crap."

He went on to say, "I believe Lee Harvey Oswald acted alone. I believe there ought to be a Constitutional amendment outlawing artificial turf and designated hitters. I believe in voting every election, in chocolate chip cookies, in the sweet spot and in opening your presents Christmas day rather than Christmas Eve."

All Sarandon's character, Annie Savoy, could say was, "Oh, my!"

That was soul talk.

My old roommate, Mary, and I used to talk "soul" for hours. Night after night, we'd get going about 10 P.M. and we'd talk about everything from Walter Mondale to the pollution in the Kansas River to whether or not her blue top would go with my paisley skirt. We'd proceed in this nonstop soul talk—which was more like thinking out loud—until 2 or 3 in the morning, until finally one of us would muster up the resolve to say, "I guess we'd better get some sleep. Otherwise, we'll never make it to work the next day." Those talks were energizing. They grew our minds. They stimulated our hearts. They made us bigger people.

We need to talk about important things. It's easy to lose sight of what's important in this culture of garage door openers and cable TV. We forget to wave to our neighbors, let alone talk from the soul. No longer do we sit on our porches, shout "Hello" to our neighbors. No longer do we trust our leaders, give people the benefit of the doubt.

What's worse, we don't even recognize the sadness of what we have lost.

People Who Live Big

JULIE AND BRUCE MADSEN
Chucked It All to Spread Good News

I STARTED WONDERING: IS THIS WHAT WE'RE GOING
TO DO WITH OUR MARRIAGE—RE-ROOF THE HOUSE,
RESURFACE THE DRIVEWAY, REDESIGN THE HOUSE?

—*Julie Madsen*

Bruce and Julie Madsen were living the American dream: a five-bedroom luxury home in Shaker Heights, a prosperous

Cleveland suburb, lucrative careers, money to do pretty much anything they wanted.

But one day, after logging ten long hours at her private psychology practice, Julie flopped on the bed and said to her husband, "Is this all there is?"

They'd both been putting in long hours. She at her prosperous counseling practice, he at his twenty-six-year-long management job with General Electric. It seemed as if their promising marriage of two years was already "same ol', same ol'." They barely had time to eat dinner together, let alone discuss the important issues that brought them together in the first place.

Add to that their discouragement with the nightly news. Surely, this cynicism and apathy isn't the only thing happening in America, they thought.

"It suddenly became apparent to me that I no longer wanted to sit behind four walls and do nothing but listen to Dan Rather give me bad news," Julie says.

Right then and there, the enterprising duo hatched a scheme. They would quit their jobs, buy an RV, and travel the country searching for the stories the nightly news ignored. Stories of hope, faith, courage. Stories of the American dream.

"A lot of my clients were depressed. And why shouldn't they be with all the despairing news blaring at us from the TV and newspapers?" Julie said. "We decided to let people know there are wonderful things happening and that America is still a good place."

Within four months, they had bought a twenty-six-foot Sunnybrook trailer and a pickup. They quit their $120,000-a-year jobs. They put their suburban dream home on the market. They sold their fine china, their antique furniture, their Oriental rugs.

"Neither one of us had ever written for a living, but so what? We decided we were journalists," Julie says.

In April 1995, the very month terrorists blew up the federal building in Oklahoma City, they set out on their unusual mission. The bombing that killed 129 people made them even more determined to ferret out hope, to find the beautiful. They called themselves bounty hunters, *bounty* meaning "goodness." They landed a weekly newspaper column that ran in several Ohio newspapers. They talked the RV loan department at Chase Manhattan Bank into running a monthly site about their odyssey across America.

So what if the journalist gypsies were only making $1,100 a month, a 90 percent cut in pay? They were following their hearts, thinking bigger than the upper-middle-class lifestyle they'd been slaving away to pay for.

Their first stop was an RV park in Maggie Valley, North Carolina. They invited everyone there to come to a potluck.

"Bring a dish and a heartfelt story," they said.

It was a big success. A month later, *USA Today* got wind of their unusual mission and printed their e-mail address; stories began pouring in. For the next three years, living in their 250-square foot motor home with nothing but a couple of laptops, a modem, a cell phone, and a printer, they became collectors of the good. They traveled to all fifty states, collected stories for their newly minted column, and eventually wrote a book with ninety-five stories of hope.

As they suspected, they found good news and good people everywhere—a priest who cleared a swamp with a chainsaw to build a soccer field for kids, a paraplegic who pilots hot air balloons, a woman who plays honky-tonk piano in nursing homes, an artist who makes crosses for unmarked graves.

They didn't even have to look very hard. "The stories found us," Bruce said "We found them standing in line at the post office or in the Laundromat."

"We called these stories pennies for heaven," Julie said. "It renewed our faith in America, our zest for life. I think if I hadn't made the trip, I might have lost a large part of my capacity to love."

Today, the Madsens are living in San Francisco, writing books and proving once again that if you jump out of the box and commit to a bigger life, the world will say "Yes" and support you.

People Who Live Big

ANDREA CAMPBELL
Saying "Yes" to Every Possibility

To create the life you deserve, you have to go after it. The universe you inhabit flows from you— you don't flow from it. Whatever steps you need to take to create the universe of your choice, you will have to push past predictable feelings of shyness and fear to take them. Don't let embarrassment prevent you from going after what you want. It's absolutely self-defeating. The worst that can happen is that you get rejected by one person—so what? You have other frontiers, other territories to conquer. Keep the big picture in mind. That's all that really counts.

—*Georgette Mosbacher*

Andrea Campbell keeps that quote taped to her computer. So far, it's working. Had she let embarrassment prevent her from going after what she wanted, she'd have never been a flight attendant, a home builder, a lounge singer, a monkey trainer, an advocate for foreign exchange students, a forensic scientist, and now, in her eighth career, a successful author.

"I follow my passion wherever it takes me," says the fifty-two-year-old mother of two grown sons.

She thinks big—always and in every situation. And she's able to do this, she says, "because she got over herself."

It all happened during her fourth facial reconstruction surgery. Not only had she developed a very rare Pindborg tumor that destroyed 40 percent of her jaw, but because doctors had to remove part of her hip bone to rebuild her jaw, she had to learn to walk ... *again*. She'd already mastered walking twice—as a toddler and when she was twenty-two after breaking her ankle in flight training school.

"I was riding a bike. It flipped. I looked down at my leg and the back of my shoe was staring at me," she says. She spent six months in a cast and, because of the pain, got addicted to morphine. When she took off the cast, not only did she have to rebuild her withered leg and relearn to walk, but she had to kick morphine.

So here she was, missing part of her hip bone, and she was going to have to do it all again. Only this time, she says, because of her missing jaw bone, she looked like she was "morphing into a duck," not to mention the fact that she and her husband had to re-mortgage their home just to pay for all the surgeries.

Needless to say, she was feeling a little sorry for herself. "When something traumatic happens to you health-wise, you look at healthy people with envy and you have the tendency to say, 'Why me?'" Andrea says.

She was sitting in a Dallas surgeon's office waiting room when the big "A-ha" happened. The surgeon's specialty was children with congenital birth defects, kids who had suffered a lifetime of disfigurement. There, sitting next to her, were twenty Russian children with major deformities.

"One girl had an eye on her forehead, another boy had four nostrils with nothing on top, and it suddenly hit me: What is my problem?" she says. "I could no longer feel sorry for myself."

That was a real turning point. She came to realize that looks and power and sex, the things most of us in this culture hold in high regard, mean absolutely nothing.

And she has spent the rest of her life proving just that. For one thing, she put her heart and soul into her writing. Her books (number seven debuted this spring) cover a wide variety of topics from great party games to self-therapy through journal writing to the criminal justice system.

It was during her stint writing for a children's career magazine that her primary passion came into focus. While interviewing M. J. Willard, a female primatologist who started a nonprofit organization called Helping Hands, she became interested in the capuchin monkeys the group trains to assist quadriplegics. Like the seeing eye dog program that helps blind people, Helping Hands trains monkeys, the kind who carry cups for organ grinders, comb hair, insert videos, and stick things in the microwave.

And most important, Andrea says, they give hugs.
Within eight months, Andrea became a foster mom to Ziggy, a capuchin monkey born on Discovery Island in DisneyWorld.

"Jane Goodall went to Africa to study primates. I learned by the seat of my pants with a primate right on my own wrist," she says about Ziggy, who came to her when he was five weeks old, barely fitting in the palm of her hand.

"Primates are very special. I know it sounds strange, but they completely alter your life. They make you a better person," Andrea says.

For one thing, they could care less how you look or how much money you have. In fact, if you want a role model for big living, she says, study primates. "Monkeys love without preconceptions, without stipulations," Andrea says. "A monkey loves you because she loves you. It's as simple as that."

People, on the other hand, become uncomfortable; they get antsy around quadriplegics.

Not Andrea. She became an avid advocate for quadriplegics. She spent four years of her life traveling the country and talking about their plight and how monkeys like Ziggy can help.

"Can you imagine even a day without being able to feed yourself, brush your own teeth, without dressing yourself, walking, without hugs?" Andrea says. "A life with so much promise suddenly exists under different rules. I call quadriplegics the deep dish wounded, the silent people."

Andrea says no one knows for sure how their kind words and higher ideals will manifest themselves.

"But I have to believe that what I put out in the way of higher ideals to my circle of friends resonates in surprising ways and will eventually reach out into the universe," she says.

"All I know is that the world is a fascinating place. And the more you avail yourself of it, the more importance your life takes on."

Are you kidding me? I don't have time to "Bless Big." I'm doing good to get the laundry done.

That's the cool thing about Blessing Big. You don't have to go anywhere special or sign up for anything new. You don't have to volunteer. Or spend any extra time. All you have to do is open your heart to the people who are already there. The people who cross your path every day. Some of them you already know. Others you'll meet tomorrow.

But always remember this. It's just as easy to bless the people in your life as it is to curse them or, worse yet, to ignore them. "To the world you may be just one person . . . but to just one person . . . you may be the world."

When Aimee Bentlage was the Drake Law School registrar, she memorized every student's name and face so that when they came to the office, she could greet them by name. Small thing? Not to a harried law student.

Aimee is now a financial planner, and instead of looking for clients wanting to hoard great sums of money, she seeks out clients who are interested in using their money for a good cause. And not only that, but she comes up with fun and unusual ways for clients to use their money. One of her own schemes is taking every one of her teachers, from kindergarten through high school, out to dinner at a nice restaurant.

Minas Demetriou owns an eclectic antique store at 43rd and Ninth Avenue in Manhattan. He sells everything from Italian zebra pitchers to Austrian crystal salts. But the real reason people go to this unique store is to revel in Minas' big spirit and warm heart. Speaking in an infectious Greek accent, he welcomes everyone personally, knows all of his customers by names, and, if you just happen to stumble into his unique store, you won't be a stranger for long.

He has several big easy chairs that aren't for sale. They're for the eighty-nine-year-old retired shoemaker who comes in every day, they're for the homeless woman who also stops by at least once a day.

His store, Thrift and New Shoppe, is a hangout for writers, lawyers, salesclerks, sword swallowers. There are people from all walks of life, from all ethnic backgrounds. And Minas takes the time to make every one of them feel as if they're family. Every Tuesday, the "regulars" even bring their families to the store to hang out with all their friends.

"It's just nice to be nice," Minas says.

The other thing we can do is look into our own hearts to see where *we're* being less than kind. Rather than get indignant and think, "How dare they?" as we cringe at headlines about cops who take clubs to the innocent or employees who take guns to work, we can look at the unhealed places in our own hearts. At our own anger, at the times we wanted revenge when someone told us "Good-bye" or "You're not what I'm looking for."

Instead of throwing up our hands and wondering, "How could anyone do these things?" we must ask, "How can I do the things I do?" How can I chastise myself for eating a whole box of cinnamon graham crackers? Or harangue myself for not being more social, for not jogging today, for not _____ (fill in the blank)?

Where am I torn by my own violence? This is the only question we can fairly ask.

And while we ask, we can keep helping strangers carry their

groceries, keep buying 29-cent valentines for kids in the emergency room, keep giving our lunches to the old men in refrigerator boxes.

3 Big ?s

WHATEVER THERE BE OF PROGRESS IN LIFE COMES
NOT THROUGH ADAPTATION BUT THROUGH DARING,
THROUGH OBEYING THE BLIND URGE.

—*Henry Miller*

The average size of a new home built in America has grown by 33 percent in the last thirteen years. Do we really need bigger homes? Maybe we should strive for 33 percent bigger hearts. Other miracle questions:

1.
What could I do to brighten my family's life?

2.
If I were to die tomorrow, what would I do tonight?

3.
What special wish could I make come true for someone today?

Boot Camp for the Soul

Happy Talk, or How to Overcome the "Fear of People" Syndrome

MY GOAL IS TO SAY OR DO AT
LEAST ONE OUTRAGEOUS THING EVERY WEEK.

—*Maggie Kuhn, founder of the Gray Panthers*

Assignment: Talk to at least three new people every day for seven days.

This week you're going to make contact with everyone who comes within five feet of you. You can smile, wink, or ask them which of the Three Stooges they like best.

You also have to talk to at least three new people every day and wave at every car you see.

Sound silly? Do it anyway. If you need to, remind yourself that the root word of *silly* is *sillig,* which means "blessing."

And the "silliest" part of all this is that these simple acts of connecting with your fellow humans have the power to solve depression, cure disease, and end world hunger. Think about it! Would you ever let someone you know starve?

The majority of adults in this country are lonely and isolated. Your big smile and crazy polls may be the only conversation they get all day.

Leo Buscaglia tells this story about an evening with friends in a San Francisco bar:

> The conversation was animated. We were all sharing reactions to a wondrous day's diversion. I saw a gentleman at a

nearby table, sitting alone, staring at his half-filled cocktail glass. "Why don't we ask him to join us?" I said. "He seems so alone. I know what it's like to be alone in a room full of people."

"Leave him be," was the consensus of the others. "Perhaps he wants to be alone."

"That's fine, but if I ask, at least he'll have a choice."

I approached the gentleman and questioned whether he would like to join us or if he would prefer being alone. His eyes lit up with surprise. He was a visitor from Germany, and he told us that he had traveled the entire length of the United States without speaking to anyone except hotel receptionists, tour guides, and waiters.

And have you looked in a phone book lately? There are thousands, maybe million of names and numbers of friends you haven't met yet. And those are just the people in your own hometown.

You don't have to strike up a long-winded conversation, but when you begin talking to people (even if it's just taking a poll to see which *Star Trek* they like best), you start to notice a funny little secret. People like to be talked to. They like friendly, funny people. They like you.

Living Big Initiation

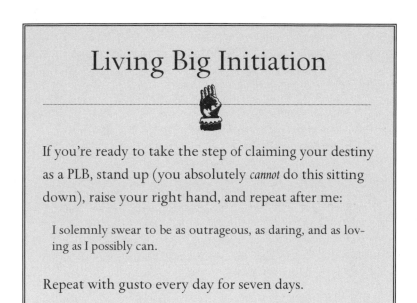

If you're ready to take the step of claiming your destiny as a PLB, stand up (you absolutely *cannot* do this sitting down), raise your right hand, and repeat after me:

I solemnly swear to be as outrageous, as daring, and as loving as I possibly can.

Repeat with gusto every day for seven days.

CHAPTER 4

Making a Big Difference: The Attitude of Commitment

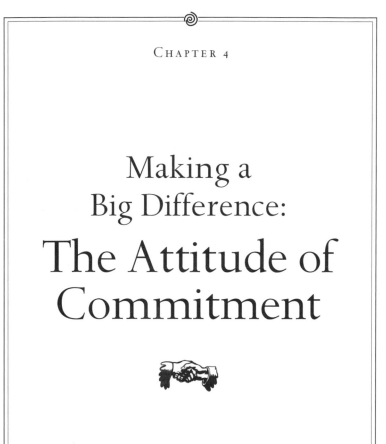

ALL OF US ARE ACTIVISTS WHETHER
WE REALIZE IT OR NOT.

—Julia Butterfly Hill

chool violence has increased 41 percent in the last five years. Forty thousand people die every day from hunger—the equivalent of a fully loaded jumbo jet crashing every fifteen minutes. Three entire species of life are wiped out every twenty-four hours. Thirteen million African kids have lost parents to AIDS.

By the time you finish this chapter, one person in America will have killed himself, and the equivalent of 200 city blocks of rain forest will have been burned and destroyed.

So what are we doing sitting here? Me, writing. You, reading this book. We have got to act.

But, but . . . what can I do? I read about this kind of stuff every day in the paper. I hear it every night on the news. It's nothing new.

What *is* new is that there is no reason any one of these tragedies should exist. What's revolutionary is that we—you and I—have the capability to solve these problems. And what's even more astounding is that we can sit here, knowing these things go on. Is it because we think we can't do anything? Or because we believe it's somebody else's job? If each one of us would take up a cause, believe in our own power to make a difference, we could eradicate these and all the world's problems within a year.

Take world hunger, for example. Balbir Mathur, a Wichita, Kansas, businessman, has found a tree, a simple tree with leaves so nutritious that it almost sounds like a magic potion. The leaves of the drumstick tree, as the tree is called, have seven times as much vitamin C as one orange, three times as much potassium as a banana, and four times as much vitamin A as a carrot. One tree can practically wipe out hunger in a small village in a developing country.

Not only that, but its seeds can purify water, its bark and roots are also edible, and it grows easily and quickly in poor soil.

Since 1984, Mathur has planted 30 million drumstick trees in impoverished countries around the world. As Mathur says, "Miracles still happen, but it's people who cause miracles."

But, but ... I didn't cause these problems. Why should I do anything?

It's like my old second-grade teacher used to say: It doesn't matter who left the glue open, all of us will suffer if we don't put the cap back on.

But, but ... isn't this something the government or the social service agencies are supposed to do?

The government and the social service agencies cannot solve all our problems. How can they be responsible for the cumulative damage committed by millions of individuals?

That's the bad news.

The good news is that *we* can. Us. You and me. One person *does* have the power to make a difference. And as long as there is health care that needs to be reformed, education that needs to be improved, things that need to be made beautiful, we have a job to do.

But, but ... I'm not really the soup kitchen type.

Who says you have to work in a soup kitchen? Cathy Runyan-Svacina makes a difference with marbles. Yes, marbles. She's known in her hometown of Kansas City as "the marble lady," and she uses her collection of a million-plus marbles, the world's largest collection, to spread love. Not only has she written a book called *Knuckles Down!* that features thirty-five old-fashioned marble games, but she developed a "Shoot Marbles, Not Drugs" program that she presents at schools around the country, and she created a "Kindness Marble" that has been distributed all over the globe.

After her daughter (one of Cathy's five kids) broke her neck in a car accident, Cathy and the daughter baked hundreds of the colorful clay Kindness Marble, no two alike, and packaged them with "The Legend of the Kindness Marble." According to the legend, a person with a Kindness Marble must start the day with the marble in her left pocket. Once she's done a good deed, she can move it to her right pocket. And, no one, says Cathy, should go to bed without her marble in her right pocket.

While a marble collection—even if it is the world's largest—may not seem like a big thing, Cathy has learned that "by small and simple things, great things can come to pass."

But but . . . I don't have the money.

Maizie DeVore, an eighty-two-year-old grandma from Eskridge, Kansas, who outlived two husbands and one of her four children, didn't have any money. But that didn't stop her from coming up with the big idea of providing a public swimming pool for the kids in her town of 500 people.

For thirty years, the determined granny collected aluminum cans and scrap metal, knitted afghans and made jam out of wildberries, all of which she sold for her swimming pool fund. Two days a week, she'd scour trash bins and walk county roads looking for discarded pop cans. When she worked as an extra in *Sarah, Plain and Tall,* the Hallmark Hall of Fame special starring Glenn Close, DeVore—who had answered an ad in the local newspaper calling for farm women with weathered faces—even talked Close into donating $2,000.

Finally, in July 2001, DeVore's dream of providing a swimming pool for local kids became a reality. The 40 x 75-foot swimming pool opened across the street from her small frame house, and she, wearing the same swimsuit she learned to swim in when she was forty, was the first to dive in.

And speaking of money, the great social activist Buckminster Fuller used to say that if all the world's wealth were divided equally among all persons on Earth, each of us would have $1.3 million.

But, but . . . I don't have the time.

I'm not denying that most of us are overcommitted, overstretched, overburdened. But I do have to ask this question: Why?

Do you really need to have your nails done every week? Are those reruns of *Seinfeld* really that important to your well-being?

Gandhi used to say that if he had a busy day, he simply had to add meditation to his "To do" list. Otherwise, he'd never get everything done.

To find time, you have to spend time dreaming. Fill yourself up with magic. When mystery and passion fill your soul, you will be unable *not* to find the time.

But, but ... I'm too young, too old, too _____. (Fill in the blank)

Nkosi Johnson is only eleven years old. He has full-blown AIDS and weighs less than 30 pounds. Yet he speaks out every day on the importance of love and acceptance. He started a shelter in Johannesburg, South Africa, for kids who have lost parents to AIDS.

Doris Haddock was ninety when she walked from Los Angeles to Washington, D.C., to promote campaign finance reform. Battling dehydration, snow, ice, arthritis, and emphysema, she walked ten miles a day until she stood on the steps of the Capitol and urged members of Congress to quit taking money from special interest groups. As she says, "We have a duty to look after each other, and we invented government for this. If we lose control of our government, then we lose our ability to take care of each other."

Age doesn't matter except for cheese.

But, but . . . I'm just one person.

So were all the people who live big in this book. One person can make a huge difference. We must never forget that fact. Marian Wright Edelman says, "We must not, in trying to think about how we can make a big difference, ignore the small daily differences we can make which over time add up to the big differences."

People Who Live Big

JULIA BUTTERFLY HILL

Refusing to Budge from 180-Foot Perch Saves 1,000-Year-Old Trees

NEVER UNDERESTIMATE THE
POWER OF ONE PERSON'S ACTIONS.

—Julia Butterfly Hill

Julia Butterfly Hill was only twenty-three years old when she decided to live big. It wasn't a conscious choice at first. She'd just had a terrible car wreck that knocked her skull into a steering wheel and made it hard for her to walk, to talk, to do many of the things most of us take for granted. When she finally did regain those faculties, she realized it was time to grow out of her old life in Arkansas. She decided to seek enlightenment in the Far East.

Before she could get there, she ran into a group of California tree huggers, or that's what she might have called them back in

Arkansas. While wandering California's lost coast, the longest stretch of non-paved land in the lower Forty-Eight, she began to feel a kindred spirit with the giant redwood trees. She felt moved by their beauty and strength. She began to hear a voice that hinted that, rather than India, her destiny lay somewhere in these old growth forests.

When she heard that Pacific Lumber was planning to turn a whole grove of thousand-year-old redwoods into somebody's backyard deck, she decided to take action.

On December 10, 1997, at an age when most girls are either launching careers or marriages or maybe even motherhood, she kissed the ground good-bye and climbed 180 feet into a giant redwood tree. By the light of a full moon, using rock-climbing equipment that she'd never seen, let alone used before, she climbed the equivalent of eighteen stories up to a six-foot by eight-foot platform. She vowed to stay there until Pacific Lumber Company and its big daddy, Maxxum Corporation, agreed to spare the life of that tree.

All alone, she sat on this tiny platform for two years and eight days. She used a margarine tub for a toilet, candles for light, and a one-burner propane stove to cook meals.

Her only companionship was a small group of support staff who hiked the two miles over rough terrain every few days or so. Using a pulley tied to a bucket, they replenished her supplies and sent her news of the corporation's growing anger.

She braved 90 mph winds, frostbite, climbing policemen with bullhorns, and most of all, repeated eviction threats by the powerful Maxxum Corporation, which seemed to think clear-cutting the redwood giants was their economic right.

So what if those trees were here before Christopher Columbus was even born? So what if only 3 percent of the

2 million acres of giant trees are left? So what if on January 1, 1998, that clear-cutting created a landslide that destroyed seven families' homes? So what if they've violated 250 acts of the California Forest Protection Act? So what if Chile had the foresight to declare their alerce trees, the equivalent of California's redwoods, as sacred, disallowing anyone to cut them no matter where they're found. We're Americans, gosh dernit, where making money is our inevitable right.

But Julia Butterfly Hill is also an American, and she has the right to follow her heart, to create an act of civil disobedience if that's what it takes.

It was lonely at first, scary even, living all alone on a tiny platform protected by nothing but tarps. She kept herself occupied by writing poems on the back of food boxes, getting exercise by climbing around the tree's branches. She claims the tree, which she named Luna, became her best friend, talking to her, counseling her to "bend and flow," and even crying large volumes of sap as it watched its sisters and brothers being murdered for the sake of mass consumerism.

Hill's refusal to live small became a springboard for others. She attracted such celebrities as Woody Harrelson, Bonnie Raitt, and Joan Baez, who trekked the two miles into the forest to visit. Eventually, she became a celebrity in her own right, granting interviews on her solar-powered cell phone to everyone from *Newsweek* to CNN. *George* magazine eventually picked her as one of 1999's ten most influential people, and Robert Duvall bought film rights to her book, *The Legacy of Luna.*

When we decide to live big, lots of things happen.

From Hill's act of love—that's what she calls it—she was able to save Luna's life. When she finally came down, on December 17, 1999, the Maxxum Corporation agreed to spare

Luna and the 2.9 acres around her. To further her work, Hill started a foundation called Circle of Life that promotes harmonious living with nature.

People Who Live Big

MAUREEN KUSHNER

Always Looking for the Highest Potential

THERE WILL NEVER BE PEACE IN THE WORLD UNLESS PEOPLE SEE THE HOLINESS, AND THE MAGIC AND THE WARMTH AND THE BEAUTY OF ALL CHILDREN.

—*Shlomo Carlebach*

Maureen Kushner has a theory. If you talk about your work after hours, you've probably found your passion. If you can't wait to punch out, consult the clock every few minutes to check if it's getting any closer to five, you might want to keep looking.

"Artists, dancers. They're always talking about their work," she says. "And that's how I feel about teaching. I love it."

Kushner has definitely found her passion—not just teaching, but teaching big dreams to children who otherwise might not have had much of a chance.

For twenty-five years, she taught art and creative writing in the inner city of New York—first in Harlem and then at Washington Heights, an overcrowded grade school where kids passed armed drug dealers and saw drive-by shootings on their way to class. As one of her students said, "This isn't Mr. Roger's Neighborhood."

Because many of her students were from immigrant families and spoke English only as a second language, they didn't exactly tear up the charts when it came to achievement tests. But by the time Maureen got done with them, 90 percent of them were scoring in the top ten nationally in reading and math—a leap that so shocked administrators that they retested several times just to make sure they hadn't made a mistake. Many of her students were offered scholarships to pricey schools for the gifted on the other side of town.

"I go into every room and say, 'What is the highest potential here?'" says the exuberant teacher whose enthusiasm and love of beauty is contagious.

To draw out that potential, she's often forced to think bigger, to see outside the box. At Washington Heights, for example, she taught kids to read and write by launching a successful Comedy Club. While subbing in one of the school's most incorrigible classes, she happened to notice a caricature that someone had etched into a desk.

"It was vandalism, but it was such an incredible picture, so detailed, so accurate, so filled with expression," Maureen said. She immediately tracked down the "vandal," appointed him as a cartoonist for the new Kids' Comedy Club and found other kids who liked to draw, write, and perform. Under her enthusiastic direction for twelve years, the Comedy Club produced eighteen joke books—including an anti-drughead coloring book, a backward dictionary, and Alf-Laugh-a-Bet Book—a grammar book for visitors from other planets, fifteen shows, and countless murals and posters.

Their Cartoon Parade for Peace, a forty-foot mural with cartoon characters from around the world, landed at the United Nations and in Moscow. After being personally invited to RCA Studios to watch Whoopi Goldberg film a one-woman HBO special, the kids in the club wrote a book called *Whoopi's Whoppers,* about the comedian's unusual hair. Soon a waiting list of 400 kids wanted in Kushner's club.

"The kids were having so much fun, they didn't even realize how much they were learning," says Kushner who required them to read at least twenty humorous books a year, more than they read in a typical English class. "Humor helped them reach a new plateau, inspired them to respond to a higher calling."

When Maureen first went to City College in New York City, she thought her higher calling was international relations. Her parents insisted she take a few teaching credits just in case she needed something to fall back on. To put herself through graduate school, she started subbing in the New York school district.

She was so amazed by what she found there, so enthralled by the potential in her young students that she switched careers almost immediately.

"Sometimes you see a child is so bored. And then—if you do it right—you find these worlds inside them. You see there is hope. Beyond every bored face, there's a world of hope," she says.

To Kushner, teaching is an art, and she has dedicated her life to nurturing children's big potential.

And while she is certainly proud of the huge leaps in test scores, she's even more proud of giving her students a cause to believe in—whether its cleaning up the Hudson River, something one of her fourth grade classes did with Pete Seger's sloop,

Clearwater, or conflict resolution, something she constantly works on through role playing and skits.

In 1994, she was asked by the Israeli Ministry of Education to bring her one-woman show to the schoolchildren of Israeli. Using money from her personal savings to buy art supplies, she traveled on foot and by bus to grade schools all over Israel presenting her innovative "Peace Through Humor" workshop to Jewish, Arab, Druze, and Bedouin children. She taught them to express themselves through drawing, painting, and, yes, knock-knock jokes. An exhibit with forty-five pieces of the children's work has toured forty American cities, including Philadelphia during the 2000 Republican National Convention.

No one had false hopes that "Peace Through Humor" would solve the war-torn country's conflicts, but by giving kids a creative outlet to express their feelings, by teaching tolerance and understanding through jokes, well, as Maureen says, "If even one of those kids remember that experience years from now, then maybe...

"When you start laughing and creating, you forget about throwing food in the lunchroom. You forget about dealing drugs. You forget that so and so is your mortal enemy," Maureen says. "I don't change people. I just take them to a different, more meaningful level.

"When kids listen to the inside of their hearts and discover the best part of themselves, peace will be possible," she says.

On February 19, 1995, the very day an exhibit of the kids' paintings and drawings was scheduled to open at Knesset, Israel's Parliament Building, terrorists blew up Jerusalem Bus No. 18, killing nearly all aboard. Several heads of states, including King Hussein and Hosni Mubarak, who had committed to come to the ceremony bowed out. Maureen wondered if the opening would even take place.

She was pacing the floors at the Knesset when a big bus of children from all over Israel pulled up, children from her program, children of all races and cultures. She watched, in tears, as one by one they filed off the bus, arm-in-arm.

So, yes, their parents may not see eye-to-eye, but the kids who are lit up by Maureen's vision of "the infinite possibilities of a good and beautiful and better world" may just make the difference.

Ten Good People

In the Bible, there's a story about Sodom and Gomorrah, two cities that once existed in the Holy Land. It's a pretty dramatic story. There's partying (too much, according to God) and people being turned into salt (it happened to Lot's wife when she turned around to look at all the fireworks). When God first told Abraham he was going to destroy the two cities, Abraham begged for mercy.

"What if I find fifty righteous people?" Abraham said.

"Sure," said God. "Then you can keep your cities."

Abraham came back a day or two later and asked again, "What about forty-five or how about forty?"

Again, God agreed.

Finally, after more searching and more heartfelt pleas, Abraham whittled the number down to ten.

God agreed to save Sodom and Gomorrah if he could just find ten good people.

I like to think of that story when the world seems overwhelming, when I hear about sixteen-year-olds gunning down their own peers, six-year-olds being raped by their grandpas. When I start to wonder what difference I, one person, can make.

All I must remember is that if I can find just nine more good people, we can save the world.

I dare you to stop drifting with the crowd. Enlist in a great cause. Start a crusade.

3 Big ?s

THIS IS THE TRUE JOY IN LIFE, BEING USED FOR A PURPOSE RECOGNIZED BY YOURSELF AS A MIGHTY ONE. LIFE IS NO BRIEF CANDLE. IT IS A SPLENDID TORCH WHICH YOU'VE GOT TO HOLD UP FOR THE MOMENT AND MAKE IT BURN AS BRIGHTLY AS POSSIBLE BEFORE HANDING IT ON TO FUTURE GENERATIONS.

—*George Bernard Shaw*

In 1999, 400,000 Americans paid to have liposuction. In that same year, 12 million people died of starvation. Maybe instead of asking, "Where can I find a doctor who performs liposuction?" we should ask these questions:

1.

How can I open my heart today and better love my fellow man?

2.

How can I become more authentic, truer to myself?

3.

How can I see life more clearly and call forth more power in my life?

Boot Camp for the Soul

Pick a Cause, Any Cause

WE ARE ALL IN THE GUTTER, BUT SOME OF US ARE LOOKING UP AT THE STARS.

—*Oscar Wilde*

Assignment: Pick a hero—someone like Balbir Mathur *(www.treesfor life.org)* or Julia Butterfly Hill *(circleoflifefoundation.org)*—and find out everything you can about their causes. Write off for information, check the Internet, go to the library.

There's a branch of boy scouts in Canada called the Beaver Scouts. Their motto? I promise to love God and take care of the world.

What a grand notion. And how different our world would be if we'd all just take care of our little piece of the world. If we took responsibility for knowing every person on our block, every tenant in our apartment building. A person who Lives Big knows the name of every kid, every pet in his or her neighborhood.

It takes so little time to make a difference. Invite the single mom in your neighborhood over for butterscotch brownies. Teach her kids the words to a song you knew as a kid. Invite them in to do the hokey pokey. Tell them about your childhood pets.

Or better yet, tell them about the person you researched this week. But whatever you do, make sure you tell them that one committed person *can* change the world.

Save a Tree

Out of respect for Julia Butterfly Hill, who spent two years living in a tree, commit to doing these three simple actions that can save our trees:

1.

Refuse a shopping bag if your purchase is small. If each person took even one less bag a month, we could save 120 million shopping bags or 1.6 million trees a year.

2.

Send your name and address to DMA, MPS, Box 9008, Farmingdale, NY 11735-9008, and ask that your name be removed from the lists of large mailing list companies. It will help reduce the 2 million tons of junk mail that's sent out every year. Writing this letter can reduce your junk mail by 75 percent and save one tree each year.

3.

And for you big spenders, send $10 to the National Arbor Day Foundation, 100 Arbor Avenue, Nebraska City, NE 68410. They'll send you three trees to plant in your neighborhood.

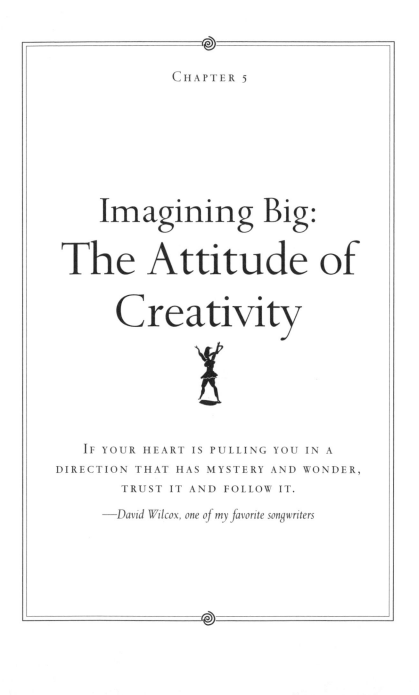

CHAPTER 5

Imagining Big:
The Attitude of
Creativity

IF YOUR HEART IS PULLING YOU IN A
DIRECTION THAT HAS MYSTERY AND WONDER,
TRUST IT AND FOLLOW IT.

—*David Wilcox, one of my favorite songwriters*

s much as I like Saint Francis of Assisi, I have come to the conclusion that I like wild people better. People who hug trees, ride Harleys, pierce their noses. People who live outside the bell curve. Either side of the bell curve. Despite these unusual affinities, I still feel like unflavored gelatin much of the time. Yes, I want to suck the marrow out of life, be Zorba the Greek. But at the same time, I want people to like me.

So I follow the rules. Mow my lawn. Watch my feet to make sure I'm doing it right.

I woke up one day to discover that my bold, creative self had given way to a rote, lonely stranger. Instead of running with the wolves, I found I was paddling with the lemmings. My zany ideas, my outrageous dreams had been left to languish in the crisp green lawns of suburbia.

I don't really know how it happened. It's like the frog and the water. You can't toss him in when the water's boiling. He'd jump out faster than you could say, "French fried frog legs." But if you turn the heat up slowly, degree by tiny degree, he doesn't even notice he's being boiled alive.

Likewise, if the powers that be tried to boil our originality out of us in one fell swoop, we'd put up our dukes immediately. But degree by tiny degree, we agree to conform, abandoning everything that's fun and original and "authentically us."

Imagining Big is about breaking free, about jumping out of the boiling water no matter how long you've been cooked. It's about saying, "Here I am." Saying, "I count. I stand for something. I am not and never will be invisible."

All of us have so much to express. We have so many thoughts rolling around in our heads, so many boiling, seething dreams.

But instead of expressing ourselves, we buy a Hallmark card and let somebody else say it for us. When the people we most love graduate from high school, celebrate an anniversary, we rely on the "experts" to express our sentiments for this once-in-a-lifetime event. It's like multiple choice. Do I want to say what the lacy card with the flowers says, or would I rather say what the blue plaid card says?

When we don't express ourselves, when we bottle up our angers, our fears, and our delights, we cut ourselves off from life's juice, from its joy.

As Rollo May said in his landmark book, *The Courage to Create,* "If you do not express your original ideas, if you do not listen to your own being, you will have betrayed yourself."

It doesn't matter if your creative efforts ever get published. It doesn't matter if you win an award or become really famous. What does matter is that you become willing and able to express who you are and how you feel.

We all sense it's there. It's why we feel lifted up when we see a beautiful painting or read a novel that speaks to our heart.

I believe much of what we call depression is unclaimed creative expression. Instead of being released, our creative energy, our very life force is imploding on us.

We are *not* being who we are. We are not fulfilling our destinies. When we don't create or express, we get homesick—homesick for ourselves. We're missing the richness, the beauty inside of us.

Creativity has transformational powers not just for the individuals who practice an art, but for society as a whole. Every time each of us increases the spiritual voltage, all of us see more clearly.

To practice an art, be it to chip a statue, to arrange flowers, to write a situation comedy, is to affirm meaning, to say "Yes" to life despite all the tragedy and ambiguities that surround us.

There's a strong sentiment afoot that creativity is frosting, expendable, unnecessary. This is the same voice that tells you you're expendable, the voice that assigns you a number, a punch card, a place in line. It's the voice of the ego, the voice that's desperately afraid you're going to figure it out.

Creativity, then, is nonviolent resistance, resistance to the dog biscuits that society wants to throw you so you'll speak, sit, and roll over.

Usually, when we aspire to "be spiritual," we think of things like being kinder, being more understanding, saying more prayers. But in order to fulfill our destiny as spiritual beings, we must also become more creative, more open to the magic, the deep vistas that gush through our souls.

Why We Don't Value Creativity

First off, we risk alienation. As much as people idolizes movie stars and bestselling authors who appear on *Good Morning America,* they don't really applaud the people in their own lives who hole themselves up to write poems or practice the guitar. When we create, we're often alone, transported to another world, a world that doesn't always include those within elbow distance. People sometimes feel threatened.

They'll say "Right on" and "You go, girl" when you get something published or land a part in a play, but until that time, they tend to cast aspersive looks your way, raising their eyebrows as if you belonged to a tribe of African pygmies.

When you create, you make yourself vulnerable, throw prudence to the wind, hold nothing back. Phil Collins compared it to going on stage with your trousers down. As long as you keep your mouth shut, nod your head at the right time, follow the prescribed "do's" and "don'ts," nobody's going to laugh, disagree, or scrutinize.

But once you write, say, or paint something, the masks come off. People are going to know. And that takes courage with a capital *C.*

It also takes courage to joust with your own terrors, confront your own truths. When you surrender to your imagination, you may just find that your truth contrasts with the persona you present to the world. As Faulkner said, "A book is the writers' secret life, his evil twin."

You might find out that, God forbid, you don't really want to do what society thinks you should. Emily Dickinson, for example, discovered through her poetry that she didn't really want to marry and keep house like her mother.

And it especially takes courage to stand up to those little voices that keep telling you, "You're boring," the ones that insist "You have no talent," and "If you write or paint, you're risking financial failure." It takes courage to rail against them, to forge ahead when they keep sticking their leg out, trying to trip you.

It takes courage to keep going when your work doesn't meet up to your expectations, when instead of getting Jane Austen, you get Barney's sing-a-long. You've got to keep plodding ahead anyway.

There's a lot of rejection, a lot of times people are going to say, "Sorry, don't want it." We must be courageous enough to forge ahead anyway.

It's ironic. We read self-help books. We moan about our weaknesses. Yet, when given the chance to make changes, to become the "bigger self" of our destiny, we dig in our heels like a two-year-old.

Think of an acorn. Inside its tiny shell is the making of an entire oak tree. It can sit around for years, hidden in a squirrel's nest or a little boy's pocket. But once the conditions are right, once it's planted in the soil, given sunshine and water, it will grow into a towering tree. Guaranteed.

People Who Live Big

BERRY GORDY

There Was No Mountain High Enough

YOU CAN'T SAY TO A DREAMER, "BE CAREFUL." YOU
CAN ONLY SAY, "THINK AS HARD AS YOU CAN, LOVE AS
HARD AS YOU CAN, PRAY AS HARD AS YOU CAN, AND IF
THAT DOESN'T WORK, LAUGH AS HARD AS YOU CAN."

—*Robert Bly*

In January 1959, a thirty-year-old eighth-grade dropout from
Detroit borrowed $800 from a family savings plan to buy a
house—not an unusual goal for a man of his age. Only this
enterprising thirty-year-old had his sights set a little higher. He
was going to use that unassuming two-story house to start a
record company.

The man, of course, is Berry Gordy, the record company is
Motown, and the plan, well, let's just say that it worked.
Between 1959 and 1972, Gordy's Motown released 535 singles, 75
percent of which made the pop charts. From a recording studio
that's barely larger than a king-sized bed, Gordy produced 60
number one hits before he moved to Hollywood and sold
Motown to MCA Records for $61 million.

I tell you this story because it demonstrates the power of
opening to a bigger possibility. Berry Gordy could have easily
settled for less. He was black at a time when black wasn't yet
beautiful. He dropped out of school in eighth grade, had already
failed at an upstart boxing career, and could neither play an
instrument nor read music.

But he had a dream. He wanted to write songs. And if nobody else would produce them, well, he'd just do it himself.

Catching a dream is the point at which all of us must start. We see a vision. We hear a tapping on our heart. We start to wonder if "maybe, just maybe, we might be able to" . . . write a song, dance a poem, leap into a new way of being. We become willing to say, "It *is* possible."

But not even Gordy could have known that when he recruited a nineteen-year-old Smokey Robinson and his high school quartet, the Matadors (later to become the Miracles), he was launching one of the biggest musical phenomenon of our times.

When we first begin to listen to our dreams, we don't always know where they're leading us. This is good news. If we could see the final outcome, we might get scared off, put on the brakes, think, "Whoa, Nelly, that's way too big for me." So luckily all we have to do for now is take that first step, put that first toe out the door.

The other thing that the Motown phenomenon demonstrates is the wealth of talent that so often goes undiscovered. Had Berry Gordy been content to plug lugnuts at a Detroit auto plant, one of many jobs he tried before starting Motown, he would have never plucked Diana Ross, Stevie Wonder, and hundreds of other poor black kids out of the ghetto. It seems impossible that superstars of their stature might have taken another path. But had Diana Ross not caught a vision, she could very well be just another bag lady on Ninth Street; Stevie Wonder, another blind kid on welfare. Thank God, they had the opportunity to tap the creative spirit that was within them.

If Gordy hadn't turned 2648 West Grand Boulevard into a "happening" place to be, "Heard It Through the Grapevine,"

"Ain't No Mountain High Enough," and thousands of other songs would never have been written.

I, for one, would have had a completely different upbringing. If it wasn't for the Four Tops hit, "Reach Out I'll Be There," I'd never have danced with Andy Gilmore at Jim Rinklemeyer's party. I'd have never known he wore Brut cologne, never known he smelled like mothballs, a discovery that can undoubtedly be traced to the tweed jacket he'd stolen from his older brother's closet, and never known how it felt to be thirteen and helplessly smitten. Unfortunately, I lacked the nerve to ever speak to him again.

How many of us lack the nerve to investigate the creative spirit within us? How many of us are on spiritual "welfare" because we haven't caught the vision? The same kind of talent that Gordy found in his ghetto protégés is hidden in the people we walk by every day. It lies hidden because nobody bothers to look, nobody bothers to say, "Hey, look what we can do." It lies hidden behind thoughts of unworthiness, behind "masks" that we put on for a good show.

Each and every one of us has that same creative spirit. But, no, you're probably thinking Detroit was different. The list of superstars goes on and on—the Temps, the Tops, the Vandellas, the Supremes. But you know what? Gordy could have just as easily opened that record company and been just as successful in Cleveland or Chicago or Omaha, Nebraska, for that matter. There are Temps, Tops, Vandellas, Supremes everywhere. There are people who are just as talented, just as musical. The only thing they don't have is Gordy's vision.

This is not to deny the huge talent that existed in Detroit at that time. What they did on that little three-track recording system in Studio A can only be described as the musical equivalent of sitting in the front of the bus.

But it only happened because one man was willing to step up to the plate, was willing to say, "I believe."

People Who Live Big

BRANDON SHERWOOD

His Magical Art Brings Out the Kid in All of Us

IF YOU FOLLOW YOUR HEART,
EVERYTHING FALLS INTO PLACE.

—*Brandon Sherwood*

Brandon Sherwood lives in the world of his imagination. He goes into this world, a playful world where everyone is noble and beautiful, dips into it, and brings it out to dispense to a disheartened society.

On a resume, it says he's an artist, a furniture maker, a wood carver. But he knows who he is. A missionary who is spreading love, happiness, and possibility. His real job is introducing people to the imaginary world, the world we all knew and delighted in as children. The world that, to him, is just as real as the painful, heartless illusion we bought into after we grew up, got jobs, and became complacent.

"Imagination makes you free" is his motto, and the whimsical creations that he painstakingly carves out of pine are really pieces of his soul, pieces of an enchanted forest that say, "Here is what's possible."

Each time someone buys one of his cabinets, beds, curios, mirror frames, or whimsical sculptures, they're buying a piece of Sherwood's Forest, a seed of harmony that he hopes they'll nurture.

His customers, who include everyone from Dan Fogelberg to John Denver, couldn't be more delighted. A former CIA agent recently sold his Colorado home and every single one of his furnishings, but he refused to part with the P. J. Trickster bunny he'd bought from Brandon.

As much a philosopher as artist, Sherwood carves his universal message of freedom and imagination into each piece. A grand-mother clock, for example, carved with gnomes, bears, and dragons, might bear the message, "Time is too precious to waste." Someday, he hopes to write children's books with all the characters from Sherwood's Forest.

Although he sells his work at festivals, art fairs, and galleries all over the country, "I tell people, 'You don't have to buy it. How does it make you feel?'"

"People need to listen to their inner core," he says. "Find out what their purpose is. Part of being alive is to go out and take adventures. So many people are just living and getting by."

His mission is nothing short of rekindling the inner fire. He hopes to connect everyone with their childlike passion.

As for him, he hopes he never grows up. At thirty-nine, he's lovingly providing for a wife, Dee, also an artist who works with him, and four kids, and he's every bit as responsible as the guy with the long corporate title after his name. But he's still a kid at heart, a kid with a fiery passion.

"People say to me, 'I'd love to do art, but for me it's not practical,'" Sherwood says. "To me it's not practical to work eight hours a day at something you aren't passionate about, something that drains your soul."

The artist from Salina, Kansas, grew up in a family of three boys. His dad, a builder and a woodcarver, introduced him to wood at any early age, and from the time he was a kid, he has always liked working with his hands.

When his dad was restoring a 1950s Old English restaurant in McPherson, Kansas, he asked Brandon if he wanted to carve the table legs. Brandon said, "Sure," and has been hooked ever since.

"I've never really had to compromise or sacrifice," says the determined artist who has made his living by exhibiting at art shows and from the commissions he gets.

"Brandon's a real treat," says Jay Nelson, a gallery owner who sells his work. "He has the fervor of a revolutionary, the idealism of a monk, and the energy of a twelve-year-old."

"I promote the journey into the imaginary world," Brandon says. "Get there and you'll find euphoria. You'll fly."

People Who Live Big

JAN D'ESOPO

She Crossed an Ocean to Follow Her Heart

SOME PEOPLE ARE BORN WITH A SILVER
SPOON IN THEIR MOUTH. I WAS BORN WITH
A PAINTBRUSH IN MY HAND.

—*Jan D'Esopo*

Jan D'Esopo was a single mom when she packed up her one- and three-year-old and moved from Hartford, Connecticut, to

San Juan, Puerto Rico. She didn't know a word of Spanish, but she knew the light and the energy in Old San Juan were perfect for her artistic dreams.

"It didn't even occur to me to be scared. Part of being an artist is being brave, and that means creating the kind of life you want for yourself," she says.

Within twelve hours of landing in San Juan, D'Esopo found a crumbling 200-year-old classical Spanish house with an afford-able price tag. Yes, it was run down and probably deserved the wrecking ball, but D'Esopo could see the possibilities. Once the home of an artillery captain, it had lots of room, numerous pri-vate balconies, exquisite views of the ocean, and, most impor-tant, all sorts of nooks and crannies where she could paint.

She paid some local kids to clear out the junk, and within a few months, she and her young son and daughter set up resi-dence. With two toddlers, it took her a full two years to get the place restored.

But today, forty years later, that rambling Spanish home is a popular bed and breakfast, the kids are grown and have their own kids, and the effervescent *gringa* artist, who could be resting on her many laurels, is still creating.

In fact, her Galeria B & B that's located on the northern edge of Old San Juan is a shrine to personal self-expression. Known in San Juan as simply Jan D'Esopo's place, the home with its quirky architecture, secret gardens, winding stairs, and uneven floors is covered with four decades of D'Esopo's art.

"My son and daughter showed great promise in art, but with my stuff covering every wall and floor, they couldn't find room," she laughed.

With seven working art studios, the B & B serves as a kind of crash pad for artists. Original paintings, silk screens, terra cotta relics, and bronze busts of Abe Lincoln and semi-naked volley-ball players decorate the guests' rooms, the wine deck, the winding staircases.

"I used to paint in little corners of the house. I figured my guests wouldn't appreciate the mess. But eventually everyone ended up wherever I was anyway, so I decided just to take over the whole house," D'Esopo says. "Creativity uses the right side of the brain. Talking uses the left side, so I've figured out how to do both at the same time."

And while she's doing it, she inspires others to be brave, to jump headfirst into their artistic ambition. As she says, "It's up to each of us to create the kind of life we want."

And anyone can, she says. They just have to believe. "Most of my guests are either closet painters or collectors or interested in antiquities," she says. "Sooner or later, guests who claims no talent will confess that they've always wanted to paint or sculpt or whatever it might be."

In fact, she gets letters from past guests thanking her for the inspiration. "They write and say their visit here was the turning point for their creativity," she says.

D'Esopo, who won her first painting award when she was only nine, took her gift of art and made her life count. She turned her corner of the world into something beautiful. If it weren't for her, Old San Juan's now bustling historic district might never have been renovated. When she showed up in 1961, most of the area was in shambles. She helped convince doubting Thomases that Old San Juan was worthy of renovation. She painted glorious pastels of the possibilities, many of which were carted into meetings with skeptical building owners.

Today, she works mostly on sculptures. "I've always loved sculpture, but it wasn't until after a big show of my paintings at the Bronx Museum of the Arts in 1985 that I devoted myself to it. I suppose when I was raising my kids, I figured it was easier having easels and paints around than a giant foundry. Paints at least are edible."

For a while, she offered a B & B portrait package where guests who stayed for five days and were willing to pose for a couple of sittings would walk away with a bust of themselves.

Today, she's too busy with public commissions. She recently installed a nine-foot full-figure bronze of Barbosa, leader of the statehood party, in front of the San Juan Medical Center. She's also partial to the fountain of Columbus she installed in downtown San Juan.

And the pastel paintings that she created when she first followed her dream to Puerto Rico? They're in private collections all over the world.

Not bad for a single mom with a big dream.

People Who Live Big

WYLAND

Painting the World's Ocean

YOU CAN'T REST WHEN YOU'RE ON PLANETARY DUTY.

—*Wyland*

It's only fitting that a book about Living Big would include the artist who's listed in the Guinness Book of World Records as painting the world's largest mural. That artist is Wyland, the mural is a 1,280-foot ocean scene that decorates the front of Long Beach Convention Center, and his story is perfect for demonstrating what one person with a big dream can accomplish.

Wyland was born forty-five years ago with a club foot. Before he was seven years old, he'd had eleven major surgeries. This hardship forced his already struggling family to move thirteen times in one year. For years, he wore a cast that prevented him from going into the water, a real drag for the avid fan of *The Undersea World of Jacques Cousteau.*

While his brothers were out playing baseball, Wyland, forced to stay home, started drawing. He seemed to have a knack for it, and his mother and grade school art teachers encouraged him to see what he could do with it. Before long, he was scrounging house paint, hiding behind beds, and painting murals on the backs of headboards. By the time he was sixteen, he landed his first commission for a public mural, an Alpine scene at a Dairy Queen in suburban Detroit.

In 1971, his artistic vision came into focus while his family was visiting relatives in Laguna Beach, California. After begging his aunt to drive him to the beach, he was staring longingly out at the ocean when suddenly, in a moment he'll never forget, two barnacle-encrusted California Gray whales rose to the surface.

"Everything changed for me at that point," Wyland said. "I knew immediately what I wanted to do with my life. I knew I would do whatever it took to make that happen."

And at first it did take some effort. After all, he was only a twenty-three-year-old kid when he went to city officials in Laguna Beach with his proposal to paint a life-sized mural of a mother whale and her calf on a beachside 140 x 26-foot wall.

It took two years of legal wrangling and red tape, but because the mural got such rave reaction (while he was painting; at the dedication by John Wayne's wife that happened to fall on his twenty-fifth birthday; and for years afterward), he made it his goal to paint 100 public murals in the next thirty years.

So far, he's completed eighty-six. He calls these majestic life-sized murals "Whaling Walls," and he donates both his time and the paint, which is no small donation, since each wall takes at least 1,000 gallons of paint.

His purpose is to call attention to the beauty and the importance of the world's ocean. "I'm not just painting whales, but the incredible spirit they posses," Wyland says. "I figured if people can see the beauty in nature, they'll help protect it."

The 64 million square feet of public art that he's created so far can be found on everything from old warehouses and sixteen-story buildings to the National Zoo in Washington, D.C., New Zealand's National Maritime Museum, and a Portland wall that he completed in 3½ days.

"I just keep looking for big walls," says Wyland.

He hopes the hundredth wall will be the Great Wall of China, which, with its width, could break his current world record.

"There's something about big that appeals to me," says Wyland, who thinks big, talks big, and has a big personality. "Maybe it's because I like to focus on the big picture."

His art stretches far beyond his whaling walls. With more than 200,000 collectors in seventy countries, this Marine Michelangelo is the most recognized ocean artist on the planet. He has also written five books and is now working with the Scripps Oceanographic Institute to create an art and science curriculum called "Clean Water: 21st Century" that will reach 67 million school kids.

"I believe totally that one person can make a difference," Wyland says.

What Do You Think?

My friend Greg Tamblyn, a talented songwriter, wrote a funny song that became the title of his first CD. It's called "Shoot-Out at the I'm OK, You're OK Corral." It starts like this:

I could tell that it was more than just a simple lover's spat
When she called me compulsive and blamed my mom for that
I yelled "I'm not the only one with hang-ups gal"
And thus began the shoot-out at the I'm OK, you're OK corral.

It's funny because he and his girlfriend begin hurling insults at each other, lines they picked up from the latest self-help books. She says, "You've got the Peter Pan Syndrome. You never grew up." And he returns with, "Looks who's talking? The Woman Who Loves Too Much."

It goes on to say:

I could tell she was going to fight me nail and tooth
When she brought up Dear Abby and quoted Dr. Ruth.

Although the song is hilarious, it touches a raw nerve. We don't turn inward. We're so busy quoting Dr. Ruth or Marianne Williamson or whoever the hottest new author happens to be that we forget to quote ourselves.

What do *we* think? Most of us have no idea. We look outside for answers. We look to everybody except ourselves.

And it's a shame. Life is being wasted. We're not having the fun we could. We're not making the beautiful things we could. We're not living, not celebrating. Instead we're following rules that some author we've never even met made up. I don't care how smart the next bestselling author is. They don't know the secrets to your life.

There's only one person who does. What do you like? What is important to you? Do you know?

Your first priority is to get acquainted with yourself. Only then can you sing your song. You must recognize in yourself an individual, a new one, someone who's very distinct from the others. Find yourself. Find the fine thing that you are. Only then will you be liberated.

Just like the acorn waiting to grow into an oak, the creative life force is inside of you, waiting to grow into a big person. Yes, you can wait. Stuff it inside a squirrel's nest. Jam it into a pocket. But eventually, it will find the right conditions. It will bloom.

Next time an idea whispers in your ear, take the time to listen. Invite it home for dinner. Say, "Yes, I'm willing to try."

3 Big ?s

IF YOU CAN WALK, YOU CAN DANCE.
IF YOU CAN TALK, YOU CAN SING.

—*Zimbabwean proverb*

In the last five years, the number of cosmetic surgeries in America has doubled twice. Maybe instead of a good plastic surgeon, we should be wondering:

1.
How can I develop my passion, intuition, and vision?

2.
How can I bring more magic into my life?

3.
When I was eight, what did I want more than anything?

Boot Camp for the Soul

Put Creativity on Your To-Do List

THIS LITTLE LIGHT OF MINE.
I'M GOING TO LET IT SHINE.

—*Christian spiritual*

Assignment: Make something every day for seven days.

It can be a poem (haiku is only seventeen syllables), a paper bag hat, or a pot of soup. Maybe you'd rather make up a jingle for a product you use. Or draw a new hat for the Cat in the Hat.

But whatever it is, you have to exercise your creative muscle every day for seven days. Jay Leno says it's like lifting weights. And just like the bicep that gets bigger with every pump of the iron, our creativity and imagination work better when they are exercised.

You don't have to set aside hours, but do a little something every day. You wouldn't think of going a day without brushing your teeth or taking a shower. Isn't the unfoldment of your dreams at least as important?

Creativity Test

There's the S.A.T. test to see if you're bright enough to get into college, the L.S.A.T. to see if you can make it in law school, the M.C.A.T. that opens doors to med school.

But here, being offered for absolutely no charge, is the very best test I know for measuring creativity in human beings.

Get out your pencil.

PAM GROUT'S TEST OF CREATIVITY

1. Are you breathing? Yes_____ No_____
Check your score.
If you answered "Yes" to the above question, you're highly creative.

Power of the Purple Crayon

WANT TO RAISE GENIUSES? READ THEM FAIRY TALES.

—*Albert Einstein*

Take it from me, the mother of a seven-year-old. The best inspirational literature can be found in the kid's section of your local library. These children's classics should be a part of every PLB's library:

The Carrot Seed by Ruth Krauss

The Country Bunny and the Little Gold Shoes by Du Bose Heyward

Harold and the Purple Crayon by Crockett Johnson

I Love You Forever by Robert Munch

Miss Rumphius by Barbara Cooney

Somebody Loves You, Mr. Hatch by Eileen Spinelli

The Quiltmaker's Gift by Jeff Brumbeau

The Treasure by Uri Shulevitz

Wheel on the School by Meindert DeJong

The Worry Stone by Marianna Dengler

A great source for children's books is the Chinaberry Catalog, a gorgeous quarterly that never ceases to inspire me. Call 800-776-2242 or write 2780 Via Orange Way, Spring Valley, CA 91978

CHAPTER 6

Playing Big: The Attitude of Happiness

I DO WISH TO RUN, TO SEIZE THIS GREATEST TIME
IN ALL THE HISTORY OF MAN TO BE ALIVE,
TO STUFF MY SENSES WITH IT, TO EYE IT, TOUCH IT,
LISTEN TO IT, SMELL IT, TASTE IT, AND HOPE
THAT OTHERS WILL RUN WITH ME, PURSUING
AND PURSUED BY IDEAS.

—*Ray Bradbury*

ne of the most radical things a person can do is to see life as a good time. To make a decision to be happy. But make no mistake. Living life with *joie de vivre* is a revolutionary act. It takes vigilance. While no one except maybe sadsack comedian Niles Crane would check the box "No" after the question, "Do you want to be happy?" few of us believe we get to choose. We think it's a matter of fate, a roll of the dice.

Did we have charming parents?

Does our partner pick romantic birthday gifts?

Does our job pay for overtime?

But those things don't matter. Whether you're happy or not is totally, 100 percent, don't-even-mention-the-word-*fate* up to you.

Maybe I should say it again: You can *choose* to be happy. You can choose to infuse all your thoughts, feelings, and actions with a paradigm of happiness.

The problem is that the going paradigm for the past 5,000 years has basically been "Life's a pain and then you die." We're trained from a very early age to put on a pair of gray-colored glasses and look at the world through the lens of defeat and pain. We get brownie points for finding problems.

Focusing on the good in life and assuming the best outcome sounds dangerously like "not facing up to reality." There's a bias against too much optimism and happiness.

Pioneer Leo Buscaglia, who taught a college class and wrote a bestseller about love, said people accuse him of being a "naive kook" because he enthusiastically proclaims the world is wonderful.

"They think I'm a nutcase because I say 'Hi' and 'Have a nice day' to everyone," he says. "The other day my flight was canceled. I said to the other passengers, 'Great, let's all stick together. We can have a party.' They ran from me as if I had a disease. They were much too busy grumbling to waste their time on fun."

The news media, of course, thinks it's their sworn duty to come up with heart-wrenching headlines. Reporters are rewarded for ferreting out the tragic, digging up the tormented, and telling us about the ugly.

Even therapists who purport to brighten our lives encourage us to dig up old baggage and peek at creaky skeletons lurking in our subconscious closets. They pat us on the back for noticing where we're stuck, for paying attention to how we are suffering.

If we want to live big, we have simply got to quit focusing on what is wrong. Especially when there is so much beauty and love in the world.

Is the guy who blew up the building anymore real or newsworthy than the hundreds of people who spent twenty-four hours digging through the rubble? Are the "needs-to-improve" marks on your job evaluation more accurate than the "doing a great job" areas of your work life? Why do we insist on focusing on the negative?

We've become so accustomed to living in the "Life's a pain" paradigm that it never occurs to us that another reality, a happy reality, is possible. Pain, loneliness, and fear are the context within which we live our lives. We're so conditioned to wallow in misery that the concept of life as a joyous adventure seems impossible or even unnatural.

Sure, we can buy that there will be happy events. In fact, we look forward to things like holidays and birthdays and time off work. But to believe that our happiness is possible 24-7 is a pretty big stretch for most of us.

But remember that's what we're trying to do here. To stretch. To get bigger.

In fact, the "Life's a pain" paradigm is really nothing but a bad habit, a rut we've been in since the first time our parents told us to "act our age." Looking for pain is nothing but a grossly irresponsible way of looking at the world.

That's not to say negative things won't happen. Life is full of challenges. That's what makes it so rich. But we always have the choice to view our circumstances from a paradigm of possibility rather than an "Oh no, not again" attitude.

Look at Victor Frankl, the Austrian psychiatrist. He was thrown in Jewish prison camps at the prime of his life. His parents, his brother, his beloved wife all perished at the hands of

Nazi soldiers. Except for his sister, he lost every one who was dear to him. On top of that, he suffered near-daily torture and innumerable indignities, never knowing from one day to the next whether he would be sent to the ovens or spared so he could shovel out the ashes of those who were.

One day, while naked and alone in his squalid cell, it suddenly hit him: No matter what the Nazis did to him, they could not take away the last of his human freedoms. This is a direct quote from his book, *Man's Search for Meaning*: "Everything can be taken away from a man but one thing: to be able to choose one's attitude in any given set of circumstances, to choose one's own way."

You get to choose!

Mozart is another startling example of someone who Played Big despite unbearable circumstances. Through much of his life, he was penniless, unable to find work, sicker than a dog. He lost several children to starvation. Yet, despite these gut-wrenching problems, he chose to be happy, to continue making beautiful music.

During his seven years imprisonment in North Vietnam, Captain Gerald Coffee, who wrote a book called *Beyond Survival*, maintained control of his perspective by Playing Big. Rather than focus on what he didn't have (and he didn't have anything), he took responsibility for his sense of joy, even providing his own entertainment. He sang every song he'd ever known, recalling memories associated with each song. He practiced being a naturalist by studying rats, cockroaches, ants, and flies.

Playing big is an attitude we can develop. By living with gratitude, by approaching life with a sense of adventure, we can deliberately discover and nourish a sense of joy in being alive.

It all depends on where you shine your spotlight.

Just Say Yes!

MAN ONLY LIKES TO COUNT HIS TROUBLES,
BUT HE DOES NOT COUNT HIS JOYS.

—*Fyodor Dostoyevsky*

Before entering the hospital room of a tuberculosis patient, visitors are required to cover their entire bodies. They're asked to don surgical gloves and face masks.

None of us balks at this seemingly overly cautious behavior. After all, we don't want to catch tuberculosis. It's contagious, for goodness sake. Why wouldn't we go to great lengths to avoid being exposed?

Yet, we never protect ourselves from the bad news we see on television, the horrible reports we read in the newspaper. I'd be real surprised if what you see on the nightly new is what you're seeing in your own neighborhood. The news media presents a grossly distorted picture.

And unfortunately, that picture of "America, the Ugly" is every bit as contagious and as damaging as those tuberculosis germs.

Poet and novelist Maya Angelou goes so far as to call negativity poison. She is vigilant in protecting herself from negative conversation. If anyone says anything negative in her home, she asks that person to leave. If she hears a "poisonous comment" out in the world, she's "outta there," and she doesn't feel a bit guilty about it.

"If you allow it (negativity) to perch in your house, in your mind, in your life, it can take you over. So when rude or cruel things are said—I say, 'Take it all out of my house.' Those negative words climb into the wood and into the furniture and the next thing they'll be on my skin," she says.

She prefers what Paul said in his letter to the Corinthians. They wrote to him complaining about old men who were chasing young women, about church members who refused to tithe. And he wrote back and said, "If there be anything of good report, speak of these things."

One of my favorite stories is about a guy who goes to a therapist complaining about his wife.

He says, "Doc, I don't care what it takes. I want to make my low-down, dirty rotten wife miserable. I'm going to leave her in six months, but before I do, I want to do every single thing I can to make her suffer. What should I do?"

"Oh, that's easy," says the therapist. "Every night for the next six months, tell her how beautiful she is. Praise her abilities and talents. Tell her how much you love her. When you dump her in six months, she'll be devastated. It might even destroy her."

Eight months later, the therapist runs into his former client at a cocktail party.

"Hey, buddy," the therapist punches him, "good to see you.

Did you finally get rid of that low-down, dirty rotten wife?"

"I beg your pardon," says the truly offended client. "My wife is beautiful. She's the most talented, wonderful woman in the world. You must be thinking of someone else."

Your thoughts are magic. Not one of them goes unheeded by the universe. Whatever it is you think and feel, the great universal energy stands up and says, "I second it."

Why cast your spotlight in the dirty corners? Why focus on negativity? Certainly bad things happen, but good things happen too.

A Course in Miracles says there is no such thing as an idle thought. Our thoughts about ourselves, about our world, about our relationships create our reality. In a landmark physics experiment, researchers who theorized that light waves were curvy found curvy light waves. And those who deduced light waves were straight as Billy Graham? Well guess what? They found Billy Graham-straight light waves.

So if you really want to know what you think, look around at your world. Who needs a mind reader or a psychologist to dredge up an unburied unconscious? It's all right there in living color. If you see dysfunctional relationships, finances that are always a struggle, a world of snotty sales clerks, then that's what you're spending your time thinking about. In fact, the thoughts came first.

Change your thoughts and your focus and you can literally change your world. A friend of mine who was bemoaning her dating life—or lack thereof—decided to put what she called "my wacky thinking principles" to work. She started thinking about her phone ringing. She spent fifteen minutes every day thinking about male voices calling to say, "Hi!" or "What are you doing Friday night?" Within a week of her experiment, every past boyfriend and her ex-husband called her out of the blue. On week 2, when she started getting obscene phone calls, she decided she'd carried it a bit too far, but she was convinced. Thinking creates our reality.

At first, it may seem unbelievable. I mean, how can I think about a loving relationship when my husband spends all his time watching football games, drinking beer, and playing golf?

Refuse to think about disgruntlements because you'll only get more to disgruntle about. Think about good times you've shared in the past. Or fantasize about great things you'll share in the future.

Norman Vincent Peale used to tell the story of a woman whose husband wanted a divorce.

Needless to say, the woman was a little upset about the reality of her life—especially since her beloved husband quit coming home after work. But rather than buy into "the negative," she decided to try a little experiment. Every night, she'd sit next to his chair by the fire, imagining that he was there telling her stories about work, about his childhood—the way he used to when they were still "in love." At dinner, she'd set his place, serve him dinner (even though he wasn't there), and continue thinking good, loving thoughts.

Lo and behold, she eventually looked over and he *was* there. Her beloved husband was back and madly in love with her again.

The word *abracadabra*—you know, that phrase that magicians use to pull rabbits out of hats—is actually an Aramaic phrase that translates to "I will create as I speak."

From now on, remember that what you say and think holds magic. Choose to think big things, things that are good and beautiful, noble and true.

People Who Live Big

PATCH ADAMS
Laughing His Way to Health

WEARING A RED RUBBER CLOWN NOSE
EVERYWHERE I GO HAS CHANGED MY LIFE.

—*Patch Adams*

One of my mentors is Patch Adams, the doctor whose life was made into a 1998 movie starring Robin Williams. Not only has Patch turned the medical profession upside down and sideways, but at Gesundheit Institute, his innovative medical center in West Virginia, he takes the most expensive service in America—medical care—and gives it away free.

Patch calls himself a student of life, of happy life. He has spent most of his adult life formulating a philosophy of happiness, about its importance and how it can be developed.

But it wasn't always that way. In fact, it was only after a two-week stint in a psychiatric ward that he found his true calling for Playing Big.

He was born an Army brat, moving every few years to new schools, new countries. When he was sixteen, his dad died suddenly, sending him into a grief-filled tailspin. His mom moved the family back to suburban Virginia, where he latched on to his uncle, a lawyer and an independent thinker in a society of conformists.

At school, he turned his grief into rage, writing scathing articles against segregation, war, and religious hypocrisy. He also wrote long, sappy poems. He joined the jazz club, went to coffeehouses, shot pool.

By the end of his senior year, Patch had ulcers. That was bad enough, but the next year, when he was a freshman in college, the uncle he'd adopted as a surrogate father committed suicide, and Patch's girlfriend dumped him. He dropped out of school, began obsessing about suicide.

Every day, he went to a cliff near the college and wrote epic poetry to the departed girlfriend. He composed heart-rending sonnets, searching for just the right words that would convince her to see the error of her ways and take him back.

"If I had ever finished my outpouring, I would have jumped; fortunately, I was too long-winded," Patch says.

Finally, after one last unsuccessful plea to Donna, the girlfriend, he trudged six miles in the snow to his mother's doorstep.

"I'm trying to kill myself," he told his mother. "I need to go to a mental hospital."

His two-week stay at a locked ward in Fairfax, Virginia, was the turning point in his life. But it wasn't the doctors who helped him, he says, but his friends and family, and most important his roommate, Rudy.

Rudy was a basket case. He'd had three wives, fifteen jobs, and he told Patch long stories about his unfathomable loneliness.

For the first time in his life, Patch empathized with another person.

In fact, a light bulb came on. Patch realized what he calls "a great personal truth."

"Happiness was an intentional decision," he says. "I had to open myself to love."

He devoted himself to learning everything he could about love, happiness, friendship, and developing a joy-filled life. He read great works of literature. He devoured everything he could find by Nikos Kazantzakis, Jean-Paul Sartre, Plato, Nietzsche, Walt Whitman, Emily Dickinson, and many other great writers.

But his best bibliography, he says, grew out of his personal interactions with the people around him. He sought out happy families, examining how they nourish joy and happiness. He practiced friendliness by giving himself exercises to do—like calling fifty numbers in the phone book, seeing how long he could keep people on the phone. He'd ride elevators to see how many floors it took him to get riders introduced to one another and singing songs. Once, he went into a bar and refused to leave until he'd heard every patron's story.

Soon after leaving the hospital, he decided to pursue a career in medicine. Because of his hospitalization, admission officials delayed his admittance for nine months so he could "get himself together."

While waiting, he decided to put his newfound happiness theories to work. He got a job in the file room of the Navy Federal Credit Union, hardly an upbeat atmosphere.

Could he turn his filing job into something memorable?

He and his friend, Louis Fulwiler, decided to make the joyless, dull job of filing into a "happening." They drove to and from work wearing kids' aviator helmets with noisemakers.

When people asked for files, they sang in a high-mass Gregorian chant, "Which file do you wa-ant?"

"Nurtured by levity and love," he says, "I blossomed. I defeated all my demons and became the person I am today. My self-confidence, love of wisdom, and desire to change the world were rooted in that brief period, from late 1963 to fall 1964, when I climbed out of despair to rebirth."

People Who Live Big

HOBART BROWN
Following His Bliss

ONE THING I'VE LEARNED. NEVER SET LIMITS ON YOURSELF, NOT IN THE RACE, NOT IN LIFE. YOU MAY NOT WIN EVERY BATTLE, YOU MAY NOT WIN EVERY RACE, BUT THERE IS GLORY TO BE FOUND IN ANY WORTHWHILE HUMAN ENDEAVOR.

—*Hobart Brown*

Hobart Brown, a metal sculpture artist, was nominated for a Nobel Peace Prize in 1998. The reason? He's made happiness his occupation. And, as he says, by "following my heart, by doing what seems to be the most fun at the time and by not doing those things that weren't fun, I think I've lived a useful life."

Indeed. Not only has this zany artist put Ferndale, California, his home of thirty-nine years, on the map, but his invention of kinetic sculpture racing has inspired millions of people to take life less seriously.

As Hobart says, "It seems to solve the problem of how to have fun as an adult."

When Hobart moved to Ferndale in 1962, this little dairy community of 2,500 was almost a ghost town. The glorious Victorian homes were selling for a song, and city fathers were thinking about tearing them down and replacing them with modern structures. There was great dissension between the farmers who had been there since the late 1800s and the artists who were turning the cheap Victorians into funky studios. A sign in a local bar back then read, "Hippie scalps. $5."

Hobart's crazy brainstorm, which eventually turned into the World Championship Great Arcata to Ferndale Kinetic Sculpture Race, brings a quarter-million people to town every Memorial Day weekend, pumps more than $2 million into the economy, and has totally healed the rift between the farmers and the artists.

What's more, kinetic sculpture racing has spread to eleven states, Poland, and Australia, and brings laughter and a sense of the absurd both to the artists who make the sculptures and to those who cheer them on.

Kinetic sculptures, in a nutshell, are works of art that move. Shaped like everything from giant bananas and twenty-ton dinosaurs to floating wheelchairs and seventy-five-foot iguanas, these human-powered vehicles are peddled, pushed, paddled, and pumped, Fred Flintstone-style. They're made from scrounged bicycle parts, discarded lawn mower gears, painted septic tanks, old bathtubs, lawn edging, and anything else inventors can come up with. Each machine is a testament not only to childlike imagination and engineering genius, but to artistic ingenuity, camaraderie, and well ... insanity.

The race, a quirky endurance contest across country roads, city streets, loose gravel, heavy grass, the Eel River, and Humboldt Bay, commences in nearby Arcata with the noon whistle and ends thirty-eight miles later on Ferndale's Main Street. Contestants sludge across sand dunes, traipse through mud bogs, and, if they're lucky, move at speeds of twelve miles a day.

"It's the complete test of a human being," Hobart says. "To do something you didn't think possible. Our joys, after all, are based on problems. They give us purpose. So I designed a race that is full of problems. In short, I designed a disaster. But I know that inside each one of the racers is the desire to live and conquer that disaster."

Humboldt County artists work months on their kinetic sculptures. They've spent as much as $12,000 and 560 hours. June Moxon has been known to peddle her 6½-foot snakeskin evening pump to her job at Redwood Bootery.

Of course, she's what you could call a fanatic. Moxon, boyfriend Ken Beidleman, and a Border Collie named Scratch spent two and a half years peddling kinetic sculptures across the country. Leaving Ferndale with $200 in their pocket (a papier maiche contribution box on the side reaped another $5,000), the couple peddled 4,012 miles in a two-ton, 37-foot kinetic sculpture. Although their original destination was Kitty Hawk, North Carolina, they changed their route in Alabama after Ken cracked his ankle.

Despite the injury, despite the fact they slept in a 6-feet-6-inch barrel towed behind their sculptures, peddled up 9,200-foot mountain ranges, and depended on the good will of local townsfolks, both claim it was the trip of a lifetime.

No doubt they'll eventually make the Kinetic Sculpture Museum, a Ferndale "Hall of Fame" with some thirty retired kinetic contraptions. Other prize specimens can be spotted in locals' front yards, garages, and even living rooms.

"Remember that game, 'Mousetrap' that we played as kids? That's what building a kinetic sculpture is like," says Duane Flatmo, an avid competitor. "It's everybody's childhood fantasy come true."

Hobart has always lived his childhood fantasy. When he was twenty-five, he took up metal sculpture.

"I decided to either starve to death or make it as an artist," he says.

He almost *did* starve to death—or at least he was about to lose his car when he approached a Ferndale art collector and offered to sell her a sculpture of a metal ram he'd welded together the night before.

"The bill collector was coming the next day," he says.

That fortuitous sale not only saved Hobart's car, but led to a friendship that led to Hobart's buying a studio, Hobart Galleries, on Ferndale's Main Street.

Hobart's notorious race, which has been televised on *Good Morning America,* CNN, and the Discovery Channel, started in 1969. One day, as a fluke, Hobart decided to decorate his son's tricycle.

Before long, the bright red, wobbly contraption had a seat for his son and a seat for Hobart and measured six feet tall. With five wheels (Hobart had to add two more to keep it from falling over), it was dubbed the "Penta-cycle" and created quite a stir around town.

"I could do better than that," joked neighbor and fellow sculptor, Jack Mays.

"You're on." Hobart challenged him to a drag race down Main Street.

On Mother's Day 1969, with hundreds of people looking on, Hobart and Mays staged their friendly, three-block grudge match. Unfortunately, both bowdlerized baby buggies broke down before crossing the finish line. Instead, another competitor zoomed to the finish line in a giant tortoise that laid eggs, belched smoke, and emitted an obnoxious mating call.

The race has been held every year since.

The prizes, like Hobart, are wild and crazy. The Golden Dinosaur Award (the first to break down *after* the starting line) gets a mounted plastic Godzilla. The Golden Flipper (the best "belly flop" into Humboldt Bay) get a flipper spray-painted in gold-fleck paint. Grand Overall (this is the highest score combination, of speed, engineering, and art awards) gets a check for $14.50.

The most coveted prize is the Mediocre Award (this is for the kinetic sculpture that comes in dead center), which is usually something like a 1972 Vega hatchback (complete with newly installed windshield wipers) or a round-trip bus pass to Lawton, Oklahoma, birthplace of Hobart Brown.

The rules, too, are a reminder that life is meant to be fun. Rule 1.0, for example, states that "it is legal to get assist from water, wind, sun, gravity and friendly extraterrestrials if introduced to judges prior to the race."

Rule 9.01, the so-called mom's rule, states that if a contestant is pregnant and in labor, she may be excused for a reasonable length of time (an hour or so) without penalty. However, the contestant must return with a glossy 8 x 10 of the said newborn for publicity purposes. And Rule 10.0 of kinetic sculpture racing pretty much sums up the race and why Hobart has been nominated for the Nobel Peace Prize:

"It is mandatory that all sculptors, pilots, pit crew, spectators, law enforcers and even innocent bystanders put great effort into having fun for it is such craziness that keeps us sane."

"So I have to ask myself," says Hobart, who just turned sixty-seven, "have I wasted my life, playing away the years, having fun? I can say now that I honestly don't think so."

Neither do I, Hobart

But, but...

I don't care what the excuse is, you're the only one who can decide if your glass is half-empty or half-full. Enthusiastic, childlike joy is not something you need to grow out of. One of the greatest ways to serve your fellow man is to figure out a way to enjoy yourself and to let people know that enjoying yourself is a good thing.

Vow today to approach your life with a sense of aliveness. Intentionally decide that you're only going to look for the good and concentrate on the beautiful.

When you decide to practice the attitude of happiness, boredom turns into exploration. Canceled flights turn into a party. Waiting in line becomes a great opportunity to meet new people. Vacuuming the floor is a ballet performed to Van Morrison. And, of course, a rainy day calls for an indoor picnic with five kinds of cheese.

Make this revolutionary attitude switch now. Your *joie de vivre* will be contagious. Maybe you'll even make the 6 o'clock news.

3 Big ?s

IF YOU'RE NOT PISSING A FEW PEOPLE OFF, RAISING A
FEW EYEBROWS, YOU'RE NOT LIVING BIG ENOUGH.

—*Erin Brockovich*

Last year, we spent $40 billion on weight loss products, 98 per-
cent of which did absolutely no good. To give you some perspective, with $40 billion, we could give a million dollars a *day*
to a worthwhile cause for the next eighty-five years. Maybe
instead of looking for the next big diet, we should ask:

1.
What is the one thing that makes
me want to get on the table and dance?

2.
What do I ache for?

3.
How can I inject surprise, fun,
and outrageousness into this day?

Boot Camp for the Soul

Take Up Singing

WHAT ARE THE BEST THINGS AND WORST THINGS
IN YOUR LIFE AND WHEN ARE YOU GOING TO GET
AROUND TO WHISPERING THEM OR SHOUTING THEM?

—*Ray Bradbury*

Assignment: Learn a song and sing it every day for seven days.
After you've mastered it, find someone (your family perhaps?)
to sing it with you.

At this point in your adult life, you'd probably rather slit
your veins in a warm bath than sing in public. In the shower—
well, maybe—but, as far as you're concerned, musical ability
was like the fabled tortoise: it left you in the dust years ago.

Besides, what does singing have to do with anything?

That's what people before the 1690s thought about reading
and writing. Back then, it was a preposterous idea that everyone
should read and write. That was something only the elite did.

Singing—especially with other people—has to do with
reclaiming your power and making the most of who you are.
Singing is a simple extension of who you are as a human being.

"Music is simply joyful soundmaking, a celebration of movement and dance. It's part of a ritual honoring life," says David
Darling, a former cellist with the Paul Winter Consort.

Like so many things, we've cut off this part of ourselves that
loves to sing. We were told by well-meaning teachers that our
middle C was off-tune and that our exuberant meter didn't mesh
with the quartet. Once again, we shut off part of the electricity.

Singing is a way of regaining our sense of play. It's a way of connecting with dimensions of ourselves that we've lost. Music speaks to every heart and enriches every life. In a sense, it's a universal language.

By singing together, we can bind our broken spirits back together. If every family began their day with singing, it would be one of the greatest services to society.

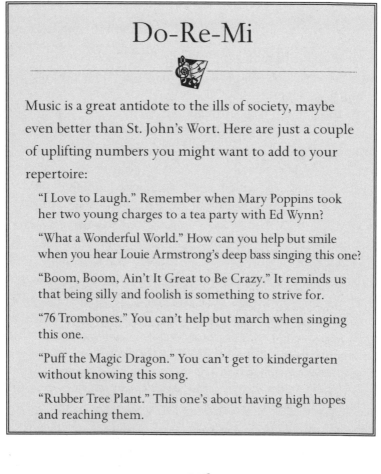

Do-Re-Mi

Music is a great antidote to the ills of society, maybe even better than St. John's Wort. Here are just a couple of uplifting numbers you might want to add to your repertoire:

"I Love to Laugh." Remember when Mary Poppins took her two young charges to a tea party with Ed Wynn?

"What a Wonderful World." How can you help but smile when you hear Louie Armstrong's deep bass singing this one?

"Boom, Boom, Ain't It Great to Be Crazy." It reminds us that being silly and foolish is something to strive for.

"76 Trombones." You can't help but march when singing this one.

"Puff the Magic Dragon." You can't get to kindergarten without knowing this song.

"Rubber Tree Plant." This one's about having high hopes and reaching them.

Raise Your Voice for Goodness

Yes, this is a form letter. Send a copy to the editor of your local newspaper. Either write it out in long hand, head to the nearest copy shop or, if you prefer, go ahead and rip it out of the book. It's time we people of the light spoke up.

Editor

(Fill in the name and address of your newspaper)

_____

_____

_____

Dear Editor:
I just thought you should know that while you were busy reporting about murder, mayhem, and other madness, there were 24 second-graders saving pennies for their classmate with leukemia, there were 14 volunteers serving beef stew to the homeless, 30 people marching for peace, and countless other random acts of kindness and senseless beauty.

I, for, one believe that if we didn't pay so much attention to the "bad news" reports and kept our faith in the beauty and immensity within human souls, there would no longer be "bad news" to report.

All I ask is that you give goodness equal time.

Your loyal reader,

(Your name)

CHAPTER 7

Loving Big:
The Attitude
of Spirituality

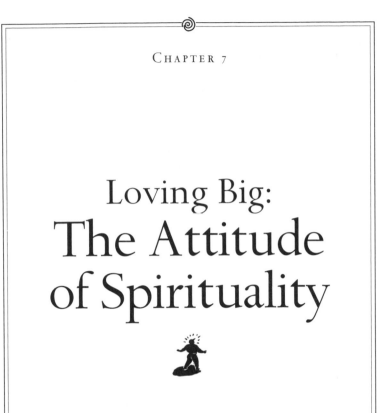

TO CHEAT ONESELF OUT OF LOVE IS THE
MOST TERRIBLE DECEPTION. IT IS AN ETERNAL
LOSS FOR WHICH THERE IS NO REPARATION,
EITHER IN TIMEOR IN ETERNITY.

—*Søren Kierkegaard*

herapists tell us that until we root out the deep, dark recesses of our unconscious minds, it is impossible to reach self-fulfillment. A fully realized person, they say, must dig for the hidden secrets that make him feel unworthy, must dive for the past cruelties inflicted by her parents.

But what I want to know is, While we were down there with our flashlights, why didn't we look for our souls?

We've spent twenty years excavating the darkness, when right under the next rock was a world of wonder and brilliance. Yes, I'm talking about our spiritual side, that transcendent force at the center of our very being. This light that is under the next rock is the most potent force in the universe. It's Spiderman, Superman, and Jesse Ventura all rolled into one.

Love is the cosmic electricity, the condition that allows us to dream of bigger playing fields. The voice that constantly whispers, "You could be more."

Most of us have a tendency to ignore that voice. We listen instead to the voice that says, "This is all there is." We get so preoccupied with things that don't matter that we lose sight of things that do.

As long as we put our emphasis on material things, believe it's more important to look good than to "be good," we are destined to live small. When we send love to stand out in the cold and tell ourselves that face lifts and Land Cruisers and jobs with long titles are what we're here for, we miss the whole point.

We are spiritual beings with no other purpose than to love this world back to wholeness. That's all we have to do.

And we *can* do it.

The main problem is we think love is something for a Valentine's card. Or a chick flick. Yes, it's appropriate conversation for husband and wife. But not for a government and its people. Love's okay in the bedroom. But, for heaven's sake, keep it out of the boardroom.

Leo Buscaglia, who taught a class on love at the University of Southern California, said he and his students went through books in psychology, sociology, and anthropology, and were hard-pressed to find a single reference to love. Yet, it's something all of us need, crave, and spend long hours looking for.

Dr. Griffith Banning, in a study of 800 Canadian children, discovered that lack of love in a kid's life did far more damage than disease and all other factors combined.

A U.S. psychologist, in a similar study, followed two groups of twelve orphans. The first group stayed in an orphanage, got very little personal love. The second group was taken daily to a nearby institution where they were cared for and loved by an adolescent, retarded girl. After twenty years of studying the two groups, the psychologist discovered that all the kids in group 1, if not dead, were either in institutions for the mentally retarded or homes for the mentally ill. The kids from the other group, the ones that got daily helpings of love, were all self-supporting, had graduated high school, and were happily married.

Wouldn't you think something this important should be our main curriculum? Wouldn't you think something this big should be emphasized every day in school, in business, on Capitol Hill?

When are we going to invite love back from exile?

People speak of the real world, the practical world, as if it were somehow more sensible than the spiritual universe. But I'd venture to say that most of our problems come from underestimating the practical importance, the mighty power of love.

I went to a baby shower the other day. Everybody was going ga-ga over cute little pink booties and polka-dot diaper pails. Here this new mom was about to embark on the biggest new frontier of her life, and all we could do was regale her with "things."

There's nothing wrong with things, but why don't we have baby showers where we share our "love secrets," profound mysteries we've learned about loving children? Same with wedding showers. There's no question newlyweds need new waffle irons and matching plates, but don't they also need our warm, compassionate reminders of what love is really all about? That love, instead of something you fall into, is something you cultivate through your thoughts and actions.

Love, folks, is the big cheese. It's who we are. It's why we're here.

And if we are going to heal this world, we have got to step up our Love Potion Number 9. We've got to realize that love is a minute-by-minute solution to every problem that confronts us, both the problems in our own lives and the problems that exist on a global scale.

And if you think love is a pointless exercise, dig this: The Heart Math Institute has done studies proving that a mere five minutes of meditating on loving thoughts boosts IGA levels, antibodies that enhance your immune system, for up to six hours.

Looking for love is a lifestyle choice. Sure you can continue to fill your mind with the meaningless stimuli of a world preoccupied with meaningless things. But you can also decide to cast your rod into the bottomless mystery of your own soul. You can tap the deep subterranean impulse that recognizes magic and repairs defects.

Ultimately, it is the only thing that matters.

People Who Live Big

KENNY AND JULIA LOGGINS
Looking for Love in All the Right Places

WE ALL LONG FOR LOVE.
EVERYTHING ELSE IS JUST KILLING TIME.

—*Kenny Loggins*

Kenny and Julia Loggins wrote a book about Big Love. Called *The Unimaginable Life,* it comes with a CD of original music and chronicles the first seven years of their ongoing love story.

Together, they are defying many of the myths we've bought into about love. That it doesn't last. That it gets boring. By committing themselves to what they call a "conscious relationship," they are rewriting the "rules" of marriage. They are proving that Big Love is not only possible, but can be a powerful and healing spiritual path.

They met when both were married to others. Kenny to Eva Ein and Julia to an older man who had helped her overcome many of her childhood health issues. For six years, they were friends only. He came to her for nutritional and colonic therapy and liked the honest way she was able to deal with some of the issues he was going through. He was able to completely open up to Julia, to reveal his true self—even the scary parts—because there was no chance of sexual encounter.

Every now and then, they'd feel a buzz of attraction, but as Julia would remind Kenny, "Honey, there would be too many people in the bed."

Finally, after both came to separate realizations that their first marriages were over, they started dating. Instantly, they felt an almost overpowering connection. Friends advised them to cool it, told them it was much too soon to jump into another relationship, suggested they date around. In other words, turn their backs on love.

And for awhile, they listened. Kenny told her he needed two months. But as he began to listen to his heart, to really honor his higher wisdom, he began to believe in the power of love. He called Julia after ten days and asked to see her. They've been together ever since.

Yes, they went through the craziness that relationships sometimes bring up—jealousy, insecurity, fear. But by being totally honest and committing to the higher truth of love, they were able to get past old patterns. Old patterns that scream out to us, "If you love me too openly, you must be crazy. If you love me you must be stupid, blind, thick-headed, conniving, or not good enough for me."

When they married, they chose a ceremony that symbolized their desire to "love big, to do it differently than the normal life." They wanted their ceremony to celebrate their freedom from the constraints of social boundaries and limited belief systems that say, "Love isn't real."

When he handed her the ring, she kissed it and threw it into a flowing river. She said, "With this ring, I set you free. You are free to follow your heart, your Spirit."

He took a Bavarian crystal, the first gift she'd ever given him, and buried it in the soft, damp ground. "With this crystal, I release you to the Earth, to the sky, to the Spirit that I love and trust."

They also wrote vows that allowed them to speak out loud all their wildest dreams and secret desires for their lives together and for their own growth and healing.

"Our promise to each other has been to follow the 'juice' in our lives, our excitement and passion," they said.

They left the crystal at their sacred wedding ground in the hopes that someone who is ready for the power and teaching of unconditional love will stumble across it some day.

Someone who is ready to believe that "love is real," that love does heal, and that love has the power to make us all strong.

People Who Live Big

JODY SWARBRICK

Raising Twenty-Eight Kids and Counting

IF I'VE LEARNED ANYTHING FROM MY KIDS
AND LIFE IT IS ... WE ALL HAVE THE CAPACITY
TO ACHIEVE BIG THINGS.

—*Jody Swarbrick*

When people ask Jody Swarbrick of Cedar Falls, Iowa, how many kids she has, she says, "Just a minute. I need to count." And she practically needs a calculator.

Her larger-than-life family includes 28 children, 27 of whom are adopted, 17 of whom are still at home. The kids range in age from nine to thirty-one. But what's even more amazing is that this forty-nine-year-old dynamo is a single mom, and that 27 of her 28 children have special needs. That means they have ADHD or muscular dystrophy or they were born blind or hydrocephalic. They come from Korea, from South America, or from crack-addicted moms in American inner cities. There are times Jody has no idea where her next penny is coming from.

"But along the journey," Jody says, "our family has gained strength, faith, and courage. We have faced trials, cried together, but most important, we have laughed, learned, and grown together."

In other words, Jody and her amazing family know how to Love Big.

Many of her adopted children are kids that no one else wanted. Not their natural parents. Not the social service agencies, who weren't really sure what to do with kids who had multiple personalities or who had been ritualistically abused.

Jody stepped in where others said, "Oh, my gosh, it's a disaster," and said, "Well, here's what I can do."

Tyler, for example, came to Jody when he was seven. Not only was he learning disabled and hearing impaired, but he had ADHD and had already disrupted two other homes. He is now twenty and happily employed at a grocery store.

Jenna, her oldest, arrived from Korea when she was twelve. She didn't speak a word of English, and because she'd had polio, could walk only with crutches.

Jenna went on to college, became the first disabled resident assistant, graduated with a bachelor's in chemistry and biology, and became the first disabled nursing student at the college she chose. Today she works in rehab at a large hospital, inspiring others to what's possible.

Sometimes, Jody's challenges revolve around language difficulties. Luke and Andy, twins from Korea, ran home from school one day, breathless.

They were yelling, "Mom, get basket. Mom, get basket. We get pets. Hurry, Mom."

As she stood there, trying to decipher their limited English, Andy piped up with, "Mom, teacher says it's going to rain cats and dogs tonight. We get pet. Okay, Mom?"

Shortly, thereafter, she says, "We bought a dog."

Twenty-five years ago, when Jody first adopted Tori from Korea, she was married. She was a full-time mom to Eric, her natural son, now thirty-one.

Had she known then that someday her husband would leave her and that she'd be a single parent raising more kids than she could count on her hands and her toes, she might have put on the brakes and said, "Whoa, this is too big for me."

By taking it one day at a time, by letting yesterday go and not worrying too much about tomorrow, she has been able to raise not just Tori—who, instead of being healthy as Jody had been promised, had impetigo and febrile convulsions and was hospitalized frequently for bronchitis, pneumonia, and asthma—but Tori's 27 brothers and sisters.

"It's not always easy," Jody says, "and I definitely don't lead a 'typical' life. But typical is boring!!"

Originally, Jody's dream was to be a pediatrician. She grew up in Cedar Falls, babysat, volunteered as a pediatrics candy striper at the local hospital, worked as a teacher's aide with special children. By high school, she knew what she wanted to do. She went to her high school counselor and announced, "I'm going to be a pediatrician." The high school counselor gave her a funny look and told her, "Men are doctors. Women are nurses." So she got married and became a mom instead.

Today, she's defying that high school counselor, picking up a dual degree in psychology and human services. After that, she plans to go to graduate school.

And in the meantime, she works as an Internet guide for About.Com's Web site for parenting special needs. Working at home between loads of laundry, seventeen loads on an average day, Swarbrick hosts the Web site, offers chats, provide forums, writes articles, and in general sees that everyone gets the information they need.

Her own kids often give advice, help her provide hope to other parents who have disabled children.

"Time and time again, I have bluntly stated . . . tell me what my child can do, tell me that my child is wonderful . . . because they are and they will accomplish milestones," she says. "Although they may be minimal to society, they are miracles to parents."

"Too often, abused and special needs kids lose their childhood. The emphasis is placed on what they need to be doing or what they can't do. At my house, all kids are created equal, disabilities are secondary to the needs of being a child. The kids are encouraged to be silly, encouraged to play and laugh. Immature antics are perfectly okay," she says. "Too often, we get caught up in believing that special kids are so much work, but that's simply not true. It's a matter of priorities and how you schedule your days."

The most important thing, she says, is learning to appreciate "the little things in life"—like family dinners and Friday night movies with popcorn and chocolate chips cookies, all events the family has marked on their giant family calendar.

Or as Jody says about Living Big, "We are all limited by preconceived notions. Each of us posses God-given gifts—qualities that make us shine. Too often, we become complacent because we are unsure of ourselves. Just as often, we stay in our mold shaped by society, and when we reach beyond the 'norm,' our motives and sanity are questioned. Our fear of the unknown tends to make us prone to stay in our comfort zone, because it appears to be secure. We have to believe, we have to have faith, even when the results are not readily accessible to us. We have to step out in that faith and reach for the stars, as they are only a fingertip away."

Loving a Big Idea

When we truly love, we're transported to a whole different level. Our worries (what worries?) are forgotten.

Unfortunately, most of us hear the word *love* and immediately think of long white dresses, tuxes, and diamond rings. Our tendency to associate love with romance is a gaping blind spot. Not only are there millions of people to love (forget your quest to zero in on Mr. or Ms. Right), but there are millions of ideas to fall in love with. Millions of subjects you could become an expert at (the French Revolution, for example, or the music of Mozart), millions of quests you could take up.

Take Larry Woydziak, for example. A couple years ago, this fireman from Lawrence, Kansas, decided to see his home state. Only instead of just driving through, he decided he was going to bowl in all 105 of the state's counties. His bought a bowling ball for $1.95 at a thrift store, named it Martha, and set out. Sounds simple enough, right? But through this simple act of Big Love, he not only made lots of new friends, but he brought a lot of attention to the beauty in small towns.

His wife, Connie, snapped a photo of Larry and Martha in each bowling alley, and he even started a Web site and a journal called, "Larry's Gutter Life."

Or take Joe Martori, for example. This CEO from Sedona, Arizona, collects pictures of famous Joes—everyone from Joseph Stalin to Shoeless Joe Jackson to GI Joe. Pictures of all these Joes (Joe Kennedy, Joey Buttafuco, Joe Namath, Joey the baby kangaroo, to name a few more) are displayed in Martori's restaurant, fittingly called Joey Bistro.

Any patron who can name all 40-some Joes gets a free meal. And while this may not be a typical love story, Martori has had a ball with his unique collection and provides a good time to all his customers.

Tony Nave's big love is cooking. He turned his passion into a hilarious cooking show. On Halloween, for example, he dressed like Ozzy Osbourne's wife and made squash recipes; for Christmas, he dressed like Bing Crosby, complete with pipe.

He often starts the show sitting in a bubble bath with a saucepan on his head and cooking spoons in his hand.

The point is, there are lots of ideas, lots of ways to Love Big. Don't sit around waiting for your soulmate. Be crazy with love. Love when it makes no sense. Love in all its bewildering ways, shapes, and styles.

3 Big ?s

LIFE'S A PRETTY PRECIOUS AND WONDERFUL THING. YOU CAN'T SIT DOWN AND LET IT LAP AROUND YOU.... YOU HAVE TO PLUNGE INTO IT; YOU HAVE TO DIVE THROUGH IT! AND YOU CAN'T SAVE IT, YOU CAN'T STORE IT UP; YOU CAN'T HOARD IT IN A VAULT. YOU'VE GOT TO TASTE IT; YOU'VE GOT TO USE IT. THE MORE YOU USE THE MORE YOU HAVE ... THAT'S THE MIRACLE OF IT!

—*Kyle Samuel Crichton*

Alfred Nobel, the international businessman who launched the Nobel Peace Prize, did so because he finally started asking big questions. His claim to fame before asking these questions was that he invented dynamite and that he was unscrupulous in business dealings. When his brother, who was also a well-known businessman, died, the news media accidentally ran Alfred's obituary. After reading what people said about him, he was shocked. He asked himself, "Is this what I want people to say about me after I die?" Other good questions to ponder:

1.
How can I regain my sense of the sacred?

2.
What is the highest potential for my relationship with my wife, husband, significant other?

3.
How can I observe the holiness of this day?

Boot Camp for the Soul

Find Your Caravan

IT IS TIME FOR ALL OF US TO RISK OUR SIGNIFICANCE.

—*Dawna Markova*

Assignment: Host a show-and-tell for family and friends. Invite each person to bring a favorite poem, a special memento, a treasure they've been keeping, or a true story that touches their heart.

Rumi called it a caravan for like-minded seekers. A group of people who share a common philosophy, a similar desire to save the world. Remember the biblical promise? All you really need are "ten good people."

Start with show and tell. Why isn't this a normal thing? Every week or so we should get together with families, our closest friends, and show them some doodle we made on the side of a Visa bill or something we thought up while waiting at the dry cleaners.

Adults still think things up. We just don't tell anyone. We don't think it's important. Not with lawns than need to be mowed and mufflers that need to be fixed.

How much closer we'd all be if we stopped long enough to honor each other in a circle of show and tell? If we listened to each other's stories, looked at each other's creations. We're all hungry for community. We need more ways to connect.

When you've found your tribe, your ten good people, put your heads together and come up with twelve ways to be an angel.

An angel? Maybe I should explain.

My seven-year-old daughter, Tasman, loves to play dress-up. She puts on my heels, wraps a boa around her neck, and pretends to be me. Other times, she's her teacher or a lion tamer or the great Tazini, a magician who can make water disappear.

Just like children practice being adults through pretend play, we can learn about love by pretending to be angels. Don't be surprised if you eventually sprout wings.

Parties of the Spirit

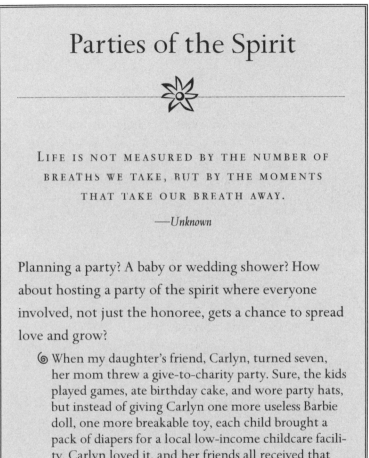

LIFE IS NOT MEASURED BY THE NUMBER OF
BREATHS WE TAKE, BUT BY THE MOMENTS
THAT TAKE OUR BREATH AWAY.

—*Unknown*

Planning a party? A baby or wedding shower? How
about hosting a party of the spirit where everyone
involved, not just the honoree, gets a chance to spread
love and grow?

> When my daughter's friend, Carlyn, turned seven,
> her mom threw a give-to-charity party. Sure, the kids
> played games, ate birthday cake, and wore party hats,
> but instead of giving Carlyn one more useless Barbie
> doll, one more breakable toy, each child brought a
> pack of diapers for a local low-income childcare facili-
> ty. Carlyn loved it, and her friends all received that
> special heart kick you can only get from giving some-
> thing away.

> Rather than a traditional bridal shower where every-
> one brings waffle irons and Tupperware that ends up
> in a garage sale, ask friends of the bride to bring an

intangible idea about love. Maybe it's a quote from Kahlil Gibran or a funny "love story" they've experienced in their own marriage. Or ask guests to "interview" a couple they know who have a happy, long-lasting marriage, and bring what they learn to the shower. That way, everyone shares in their inspiring secrets of marriage.

⑥ As the old African saying goes, "It takes a village to raise a child." Throw a baby shower inviting each guest to bring a pledge of some kind, a commitment to what they're willing to do as part of this new child's village. Maybe they'll baby-sit one Thursday a month so the new mom can have a massage. Maybe they'd rather take the child to a special park when she turns three. This gives guests a chance to really examine their own gifts (What do I have to offer?) and to join with their friend, the new mom, in her new journey.

Wrapping Up with a Big Bang

THERE IS NO GREATER WASTE THAN TO LIVE AN
ORDINARY LIFE. THERE IS NOTHING MORE TRAGIC
THAN A PERSON WHO HAS LOST THEIR MAGIC!

—Mark Eberra

You've heard the voice. The one that continually whispers, "You could be more." The one that beckons, "Make your life extraordinary."

Why else do your ears perk up when you hear about an artist or an activist or anybody doing something BIG, something truly unique? You start to wonder.

Or you feel just a slight edge of dissatisfaction. It's not that you're not grateful for your job, your car, your American Express card, but you always kinda wonder, "Isn't there something more?"

That's what Buckminster Fuller was wondering seventy-four years ago, when he decided to conduct a little experiment. He decided to experiment with his own life, to see what one penniless unknown individual might be able to do on behalf of humanity. Dubbing himself Guinea Pig B, he dedicated himself to living a Big Life.

At the time he started the experiment, he was thirty-two. He was what you might call a "nobody." Bankrupt and unemployed, he had a wife and new baby to support. His first child, the new baby's older sister, had just died. He was drinking heavily.

His prospects didn't look promising. But he decided to cast aside the past, to give up limiting thoughts. He wanted to know, "What could one person do to change the world?"

For the next fifty-six years, he devoted himself to his unique experiment. He took risks, he asked, "What if?"

Not only did he become an architect, an inventor, an author, and a great leader, but between 1927 when he launched the experiment until his death in 1983, he wrote 28 books, received 44 honorary degrees, won 25 U.S. patents, and literally changed the way humans see themselves.

That's what I hope *Living Big* has done for you. I hope it has changed the way you see yourself. I hope it has inspired you to conduct an experiment with your own life, to ask, "What is the most I can possibly become?"

Every one of us longs for a meaningful life. We all want an extraordinary life, one that sizzles, one that makes others want to stand up and cheer.

I hope you will go out now and become the most fantastic, the most joyful, the most wondrous, the most beautiful, the most tender human being you possibly can.

ACKNOWLEDGMENTS

Thanks to Patti Breitman, who took me under her wing five years ago and gave me my wings. Thank you, Heather McArthur, Leslie Berriman, and Pam Suwinsky, for pushing me to excellence (my mother would also like to say thanks for insisting I take out swear words). Special thanks to Mark Victor Hansen, Richard Carlson, Victoria Moran, Cathy Runyan-Svinca, Father Paul Keenan, Kitty Shea (a.k.a. rainbow-flavored gelatin), Maureen Kushner, Andrea Campbell, Ron DeWitt, and, of course, my ever-growing, ever-loving daughter, Tasman McKay Grout.

Photo: Ron DeWitt

ABOUT THE AUTHOR

Pam Grout is a hopeless romantic who still believes the world is a beautiful place, that people are noble, and that anything is possible.

For a living (and she always wonders why people think that's such an important question), she writes books (*Living Big* is the sixth) and articles for such magazines as *People, Travel & Leisure, Outside,* and *Family Circle.* She also enjoys writing bedtime stories for her seven-year-old daughter, but that's more about making a life than a living. She's keenly aware there's a huge difference.

In making a life, she's traveled to all the world's continents, learned fifty-nine ways to make a fort out of sofa cushions, perfected a mean tennis forehand, and volunteered at a women's prison and a free health clinic.

She lives in Lawrence, Kansas, with her daughter, Tasman, and their cat, Elton.

Check out her Web site at *www.pamgrout.com.*

TO OUR READERS

Conari Press publishes books on topics ranging from spirituality, personal growth, and relationships to women's issues, parenting, and social issues. Our mission is to publish quality books that will make a difference in people's lives—how we feel about ourselves and how we relate to one another. We value integrity, compassion, and receptivity, both in the books we publish and in the way we do business.

As a member of the community, we donate our damaged books to nonprofit organizations, dedicate a portion of our proceeds from certain books to charitable causes, and continually look for new ways to use natural resources as wisely as possible. Our readers are our most important resource, and we value your input, suggestions, and ideas about what you would like to see published. Please feel free to contact us, to request our latest book catalog, or to be added to our mailing list.

2550 Ninth Street, Suite 101
Berkeley, California 94710-2551
800-685-9595 • 510-649-7175
fax: 510-649-7190 • e-mail: conari@conari.com
www.conari.com